WORKS 7

STEPHEN COPESTAKE

LONDON • NEW YORK • SYDNEY • JOHANNESBURG • SINGAPORE • TORONTO • NEW DELHI

In easy steps is an imprint of Computer Step
Southfield Road . Southam
Warwickshire CV47 0FB . England

http://www.ineasysteps.com

Notice of Liability

Every effort has been made to ensure that this book contains
accurate and current information. However, Computer Step and the
author shall not be liable for any loss or damage suffered by readers
as a result of any information contained herein.

Trademarks

Microsoft® and Windows® are registered trademarks of Microsoft
Corporation. All other trademarks are acknowledged as belonging to
their respective companies.

Printed and bound in the United Kingdom

ISBN 1-84078-148-3

Contents

Spreadsheet   79

3

Database 125

4

Getting started

This chapter shows you how Works 7 provides a common look in most of the modules, so you can get started quickly. You'll learn how to create new documents and open/save existing ones (with templates and wizards) then create your own templates. Finally, you'll customise the Task Launcher, so it looks and performs the way you want it, then get information you need from the inbuilt Help system, the Getting Started manual and Works 7 Quick Tours.

Covers

Chapter One

Introduction

Works 7 consists of these principal modules:

- Word Processor

- Spreadsheet

- Database

- Calendar

- Works Portfolio

- My Projects Organizer

If you're using Works Suite 2003 instead of Works 7, see 'Works Suite 2003 in easy steps'.

In a sense, the first three are 'cutdown' versions of Microsoft Word, Excel and Access. In spite of this, however, all the modules provide a high level of functionality and ease of use. Another great advantage of Works 7 is that it integrates the modules well. As far as possible, they share a common look and feel.

The illustration below shows the Word Processor opening screen. Flagged are components which are common to many of the other modules, too:

Title bar   Menu bar   Toolbars

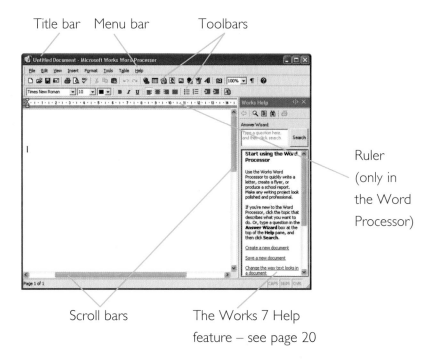

Ruler (only in the Word Processor)

Scroll bars   The Works 7 Help feature – see page 20

Compare the Word Processor screen on the facing page with the following:

The opening screens used by Calendar, Works Portfolio and My Projects Organizer are rather different.

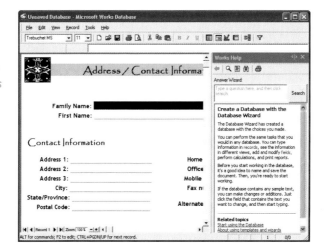

Database screen

There are, of course, differences between the module screens; we'll explore these in later chapters.

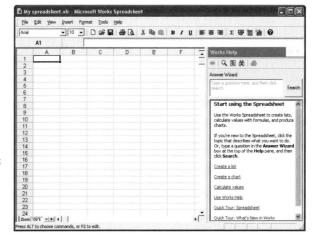

Spreadsheet screen

Notice that many of the screen components are held in common. The purpose of this shared approach is to ensure that users of Works 7 can move between modules with the minimum of readjustment.

New document creation

Because the Word Processor, Database and Spreadsheet modules are uniform in the way they create new documents, we'll look at this topic here rather than in later module-specific chapters.

Most Works 7 modules let you:

- create new blank documents

- create new documents with the help of a 'wizard'

- create new documents based on a 'template' you've created yourself

Creating blank documents is the simplest route to new document creation; use this if you want to define the document components yourself from scratch. This is often not the most efficient way to create new documents.

When you create new documents, you can use Works Portfolio as a handy repository for text or pictures you're likely to use more than once. Works Portfolio makes creating professional documents even easier – see Chapter 6.

Wizards are a shortcut to the creation of new documents. You work through one or more dialogs (usually one), answering the appropriate questions and making the relevant choices. Wizards greatly simplify and speed up the creation of new documents (while at the same time producing highly professional results) and use professional templates to achieve their results.

Templates are sample documents complete with the relevant formatting and/or text. When you've created and formatted a document (so that it meets your requirements) you can save it to disk as your own template. Basing a new document on this template automatically provides access to any inherent text and/or formatting, a great timesaver (although, unlike wizards there are no questions to answer).

Documents created with the use of wizards or templates can easily be amended subsequently.

All three document creation methods involve launching the Works 7 Task Launcher. This is a useful Internet-style screen which you can also use to open existing Works documents.

For more information on opening Works documents, see page 17.

Creating blank documents

You can use a keyboard shortcut (but not in Word Processor, Calendar, Works Portfolio or My Projects Organizer) to run the Task Launcher. Simply press Ctrl+N.

You can create a new blank document from within most of the Works 7 modules.

The first step is to launch the Task Launcher. From within any module except Calendar or My Projects Organizer, pull down the File menu and click New. Now do the following:

For how to create a new Portfolio collection or a new project, see Chapters 6 and 7 respectively.

1 Click Programs

2 Click the relevant module entry

3 Click Start a blank...

If you've selected Works Database in step 2 (to create a new blank database), Works 7 doesn't immediately comply after step 3; before it can do so, you need to define the necessary fields.
(See Chapter 4 for how to do this.)

Running the Task Launcher automatically

If you want to create a new blank document immediately after you've started Works 7, you don't need to launch the Task Launcher manually: it appears automatically.

Once the Task Launcher is on-screen, however, you can follow the above steps to produce the relevant blank document.

Using templates and wizards

The templates in Works 7 have been newly updated and organised – for example, they incorporate completely new clip art.

See pages 65–67 for more on the Letter Wizard.

Works 7 provides a large number of wizards, organised under overall category headings. These wizards make use of a large collection of professionally-created templates. With these, you can create a wide variety of professional-quality documents (Works 7 calls this 'carrying out tasks'). For example, you can create recipe books, home inventories, fax cover sheets, brochures, flyers, menus, newsletters, school reports, invitations, student schedules, errand lists, graph paper, financial worksheets . . .

Basing new documents on a wizard

Launch the Task Launcher then carry out the following steps:

Works 7 also has various email and Internet tools. For example, you can click MSN under Programs on the Task Launcher to access information services such as Encarta. Or click MSN Photos to share photos online for free.

1 Select Tasks

3 Select a task

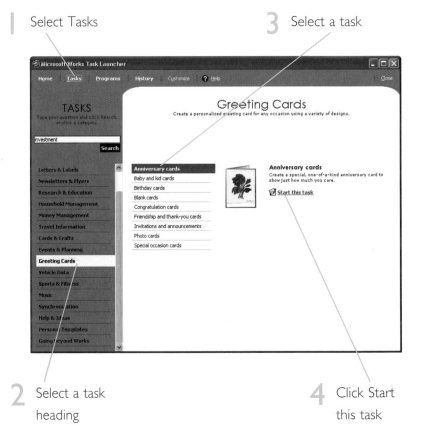

2 Select a task heading

4 Click Start this task

When you've selected the wizard you want to use, Works 7 launches a dialog which varies accordingly. However, the basic format is the same. Works is asking you to supply it with the information required by making the relevant choices.

Carry out the following steps:

This is one of a series of tasks which create excellent greeting cards – the equivalent dialog in other wizards will be slightly different.

5 Make the relevant choice

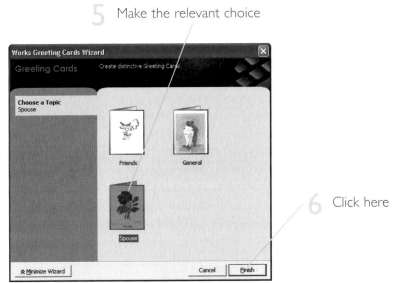

6 Click here

The end result:

Save your work at this point – see page 18.

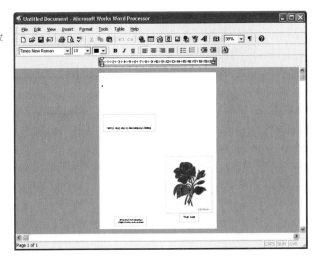

Here, an anniversary card has been created

Locating tasks

The Search box is not the same as the Answer Wizard – the latter locates help topics, not tasks.

Works 7 offers numerous tasks based on templates/wizards. There are so many tasks, in fact, that there is a special technique you can use to find the one you want.

Searching for tasks

1 In the Tasks or Programs sections of the Tasks Launcher, click in the Search box

2 Type in text which is representative of the task you need e.g. 'greeting card'

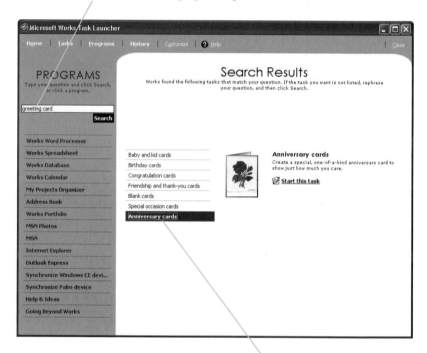

3 Works provides a list of related tasks – launch the one you want in the usual way

Creating your own templates

In any Works 7 module apart from Calendar and My Projects Organizer, you can save an existing document (complete with all text and formatting) as a template. You can then use this template as the basis for new document creation. The text/formatting is immediately carried across.

To use a template you've created, follow the procedures on page 16.

Saving your work as a template

First, open the document you want to save as a template (for how to do this, see page 17). Pull down the File menu and click Save As. Now do the following:

Creating your own templates is a great time-saver.

Click here. In the drop-down list, click the drive you want to host the template

Re step 2 – you may have to double-click one or more folders first, to locate the folder you want to host the new template.

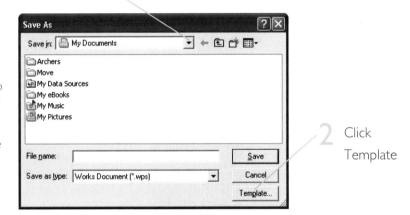

2 Click Template

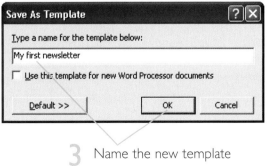

3 Name the new template and click OK

Using your own templates

Any templates you create are automatically accessible from the Task Launcher under the heading 'Personal Templates' (this does not appear until you've created at least one template).

Opening a template

In the Task Launcher (either when you've just started Works 7 or after you've started the Launcher manually), carry out the following steps:

1 Select Tasks   3 Select a template

2 Select Personal   4 Click Start
  Templates   this task

5 Works opens a document which is an exact copy of your template – amend it as required then save it under another name

Opening Works 7 documents

We saw earlier that Works 7 lets you create new documents in various ways. You can also open Word Processor, Spreadsheet and Database documents you've already created:

To open a file into any Works module that supports files, press Ctrl+O. Use the Open dialog to locate then double-click the file.

(To import a file in third-party formats, select the format in the Files of type field before double-clicking the file.)

- just after you've started Works 7

- from within the relevant Works 7 module

Opening an existing document at startup

Immediately after you've started Works, carry out steps 1–3:

1 Click History

2 Optional – click a column heading to view its contents in the reverse order

For how to open projects, see Chapter 7.

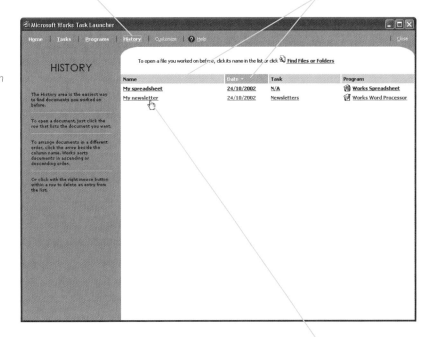

3 Click the file you want to open

Saving Works 7 documents

For how to save projects, see Chapter 7.

It's important to save your work at frequent intervals, in order to avoid data loss in the event of a hardware fault or power interruption. With the exception of the Calendar (which saves work automatically) and My Projects Organizer, Works 7 uses a consistent approach to saving throughout its modules.

Saving a document for the first time

In the Word Processor, Spreadsheet or Database modules, pull down the File menu and click Save. Or press Ctrl+S. Now do the following:

You can export Works 7 documents in formats which can be utilised by other programs. For example, you can save files created in the Word Processor module into HTML format, for use on the Web.

After step 1, click in the Save as type: field. In the drop-down list, select the external format. Then follow steps 2–3.

1 Click here. In the drop-down list, click the drive you want to host the file

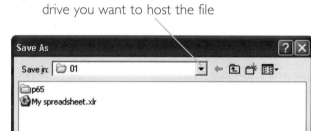

2 Name the file

3 Click Save

Re step 2 – you may have to double-click one or more folders first, to locate the folder you want to host the new file.

Saving previously saved documents

In any of the modules apart from Calendar and My Projects Organizer, pull down the File menu and click Save. Or press Ctrl+S. No dialog launches; instead, Works 7 saves the latest version of your document to disk, overwriting the previous version.

Customising the Task Launcher

We've seen just how useful the Task Launcher is: using it is central to many Works operations. However, you can also now customise its appearance to some extent. Most usefully, you can specify that it display most options as icons instead of links. You may find this more visually attractive.

The Task Launcher now has an additional pane: Home. For how to use this, see Chapter 7.

Customising the Task Launcher

From within any Task Launcher section, click Customize in the overhead bar

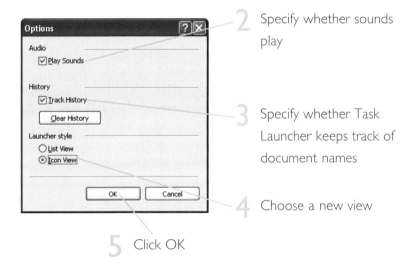

2 Specify whether sounds play

3 Specify whether Task Launcher keeps track of document names

4 Choose a new view

5 Click OK

The new-look Tasks section

Getting help

Works 7 documents can have their own Help pane, which you may find useful in the early days of Works use.

Using the Help pane

From within any relevant module, press F1 then:

2 Click here for a structured list of topics

3 Click here to search for a topic

In any Help window, click any coloured link to display further information.

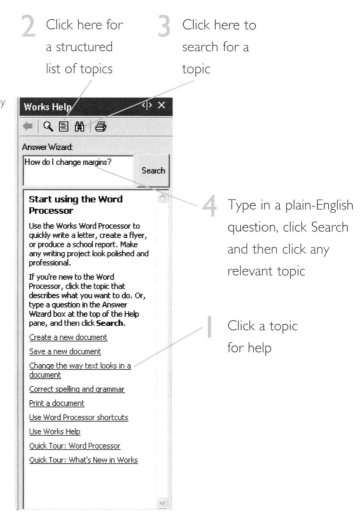

4 Type in a plain-English question, click Search and then click any relevant topic

1 Click a topic for help

5 If you want to hide the Help pane, click the X in the top right-hand corner

Using the Getting Started manual

Works comes with its own manual. You can use this to get instructions on performing common Works-related tasks.

Launching the manual

From within the Task Launcher, do the following:

Click Programs

Click Works Getting Started manual

Click Help & Ideas

Click Start this task

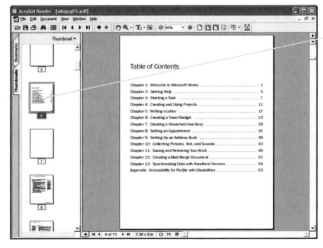

This is the Acrobat Reader – the Works 7 Installer should have installed this, if you didn't already have it.

Click an icon to view the page

Using the Works 7 tour

Works comes with a series of Quick Tours. You can use these to get information on program features and how to make the most of them.

Launching Quick Tours

Follow steps 1–2 on page 21. In step 3, however, click Take a Tour of Works. Perform step 4

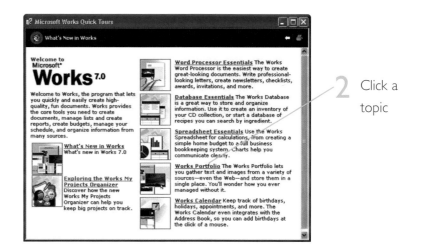

2 Click a topic

3 Click any further relevant link(s)

Word Processor

This chapter shows you how to carry out basic/advanced editing in the Word Processor. You'll negotiate the screen, enter/proof text and perform find-and-replace operations. You'll also format and align text (including via the Format Gallery), insert headers/footers and undo/redo editing actions. You'll learn how to 'round-trip' files to Microsoft Word; insert clip art, pictures, tables and watermarks; and customise page layout/printing.

Finally, you'll carry out mail merges.

Covers

Chapter Two

The Word Processor screen

Below is an illustration of the Word Processor screen:

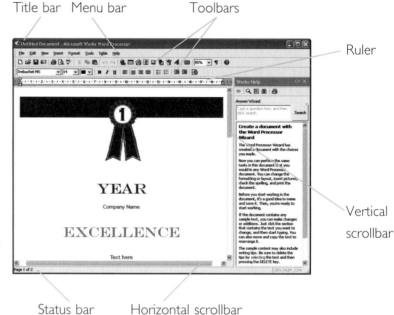

Title bar Menu bar Toolbars

Ruler

Vertical scrollbar

YEAR

Company Name

EXCELLENCE

Text here

Status bar Horizontal scrollbar

Some of these – e.g. the ruler and scrollbars – are standard to just about all programs which run under Windows. A few of them can be hidden, if required.

Specifying which toolbars display

Pull down the View menu and click Toolbars. In the submenu, tick a toolbar entry to display it or untick it to hide it

Entering text

The Word Processor lets you enter text immediately after you've started it. You enter text at the insertion point:

The Word Processor has automatic word wrap. This means that you don't have to press Return to enter text on a new line: a new line is automatically started for you, when required.

Only press Return if you need to begin a new paragraph.

Begin entering text at the insertion point

You can enter text as a hyperlink. Pull down the Insert menu and select Hyperlink. In the dialog, select what to link to (e.g. a website or email address) then enter the hypelink text.

Performing a word count

If you want to restrict the word count to specific paragraphs, pre-select them

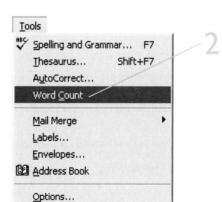

Pull down the Tools menu and click here. Then click OK in the special message

Sharing text with Word 2002

In Works 7, you can 'round-trip' files to Microsoft Word 2002, edit them there and then re-export them to Works 7.

Exporting to Word 2002

1 Follow the procedures on page 18. Before step 3, click in the Save as type: field and select Word 97-2002 & 6.0/95 - RTF (*.doc)

2 Open the Word-format file in Word 2002 itself

3 Make any desired editing changes then save them and close the file

Because Word 2002 supports more features than Works 7, some of them may be lost if you import native Word 2002 documents into Works.

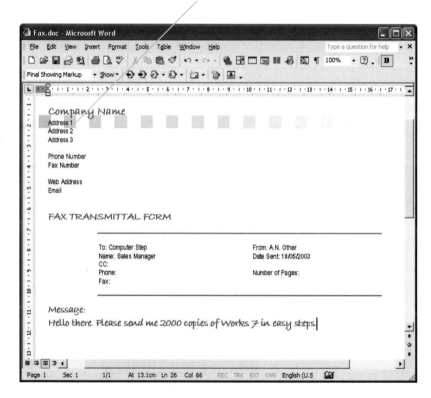

4 In the Works Word Processor, press Ctrl+O. In the Files of type: field in the Open dialog, select Word 97-2002 (*.doc)

5 Locate then double-click the Word document to open it

Moving around in documents

You can use standard Windows techniques (i.e. keystrokes like Page Up and the vertical/horizontal scroll bars) to move through Word Processor documents. You can also use a special dialog.

Using the Find and Replace dialog

You can use the Find and Replace dialog to move to any page number within the open document.

Pull down the Edit menu and click Go To (or just press Ctrl+G). Now do the following:

Ensure Page is selected, then type in a page number

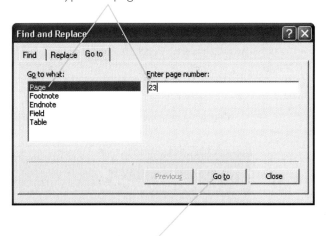

Click Go to

To insert a footnote or endnote into a document, place the insertion point at the relevant location. Pull down the Insert menu and click Footnote. In the dialog which launches, select Footnote or Endnote. Click OK. Finally, type in the note text then return to the body of the document.

You can also use the Find and Replace dialog to move to pre-inserted footnotes or endnotes. Footnotes are references or notes placed at the bottom of the page, while endnotes are positioned at the end of the relevant document (or – less commonly – at the end of sections). Footnotes and endnotes are prefaced with numbers. For how to insert footnotes/endnotes, see the HOT TIP.

Once you've inserted an endnote or footnote, you can then have the Word Processor jump to it.

Launch the Find and Replace dialog. In step 1, select Footnote or Endnote and type in the note number. Then carry out step 2.

Viewing special characters

The Word Processor has a special view mode whereby special characters:

- manual hyphens

- non-breaking spaces

- paragraph marks

- spaces

You can insert € (the Euro symbol) into Word Processor documents. Fonts which support this include:

- *Arial*
- *Courier New*
- *Impact*
- *Tahoma, and;*
- *Times New Roman*

To insert the Euro symbol, press the Num Lock key on your keyboard. Hold down Alt and press 0128 (consecutively). Release Alt and turn off Num Lock.

can be made visible. This is sometimes useful. For example, if you want to ensure there are no double spaces between words (something which happens surprisingly often), it's much easier to delete the unwanted spaces if you can see them.

Viewing hidden characters

Pull down the View menu and click All Characters.

The illustration below shows some (normally invisible) characters:

The arrows denote tabs   The dots denote spaces

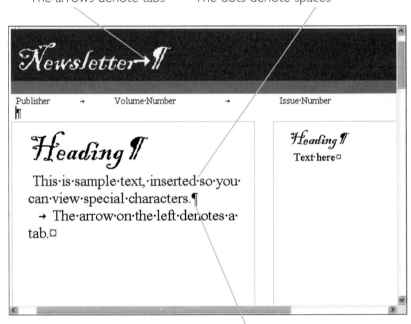

These symbols denote paragraph marks

Inserting special characters

To insert special (hidden) characters, carry out the following procedure.

Inserting hidden characters

Pull down the Insert menu and do the following:

One effect of justifying text (see page 39) is that Works 7 increases the gaps between words to ensure that the text meets both the left and right margins. This can produce unsightly results (especially in columns).

You can combat this by inserting a manual hyphen into a troublesome word. Click anywhere in the word. Follow steps 1–2. In step 3, select Optional Hyphen.

Click here

2 Select this tab

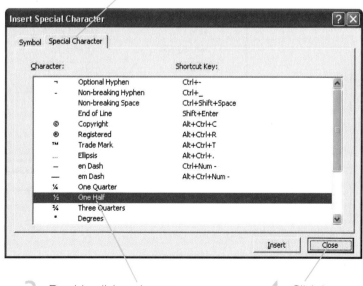

3 Double-click a character

4 Click here

Changing zoom levels

The ability to vary the level of magnification for the active document is often useful. Sometimes, it's helpful to 'zoom out' (i.e. decrease the magnification) so that you can take an overview; at other times, you'll need to 'zoom in' (increase the magnification) to work in greater detail.

The Word Processor module lets you do either of these very easily.

Setting the zoom level

1 Pull down the View menu and click Zoom

2 Perform one of steps 3–5. Then carry out step 6

3 Click a preset zoom level

Zoom [?][X]

Zoom enlarges or shrinks the display to show more or less of your document. It does not affect printing.

- ○ 200%
- ● 100%
- ○ 75%
- ○ Whole Page

- ○ Two Pages
- ○ Page Width
- ○ Margin Width
- ○ Custom %:
  - [100% ⬍]

[OK]   [Cancel]

4 Click a margin-based setting

5 Click Custom and type in your own percentage (in the range: 25–500%)

6 Click here

Formatting text – an overview

The Word Processor lets you format text in a variety of ways. Very broadly, however, and for the sake of convenience, text formatting can be divided into two overall categories:

Character formatting

Character formatting is concerned with altering the *appearance* of selected text. Examples include:

- changing the font

- changing the type size

- colouring text

- changing the font style (bold, italic, underlining etc.)

- applying font effects (e.g. superscript/subscript, outline and shadow)

Character formatting is a misnomer in one sense: it can also be applied to specified paragraphs of text, or to parts of specified paragraphs.

Paragraph formatting

Paragraph formatting has to do with the structuring and layout of paragraphs of text. Examples include:

- specifying paragraph indents

- specifying paragraph alignment (e.g. left or right justification)

- specifying paragraph and line spacing

- imposing borders and/or fills on paragraphs

Changing the font and/or type size

Character formatting can be changed in two ways:

- from within the Font dialog

- (to a lesser extent) by using the Formatting toolbar

Applying a new font or type size via a dialog

First, select the text whose typeface and/or type size you want to amend. Pull down the Format menu and click Font. Now carry out steps 1 and/or 2 below. Finally, follow step 3:

You can also apply various styles (Bold, Italic or both) to text, though they may not all be available for a given font. Just click in the Font style field and make a choice. Or use the following keyboard shortcuts:

Ctrl+B   Emboldens text

Ctrl+I   Italicises text

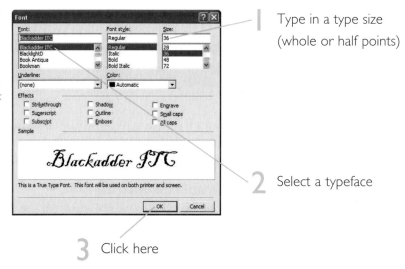

1 Type in a type size (whole or half points)

2 Select a typeface

3 Click here

Applying a new font or type size via the toolbar

Make sure the Formatting toolbar is visible. Now select the text you want to amend and do the following:

If the Formatting toolbar isn't currently visible, pull down the View menu and click Toolbars, Formatting.

Click here; select the font you want to use in the drop-down list

Type in the type size you need and press Enter

Changing text colour

You can change the colour of text by using the Font dialog, or via the Formatting toolbar.

Colouring text via a dialog

First, select the text you want to alter. Pull down the Format dialog and click Font. Now do the following:

Click here

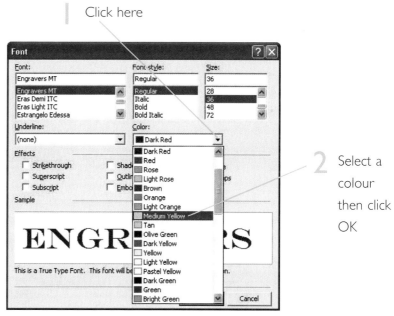

Select a colour then click OK

Re step 2 – selecting Automatic in the colour list sets the colour to black (unless you've amended the default Windows text colour).

Colouring text via the toolbar

Make sure the Formatting toolbar is visible. Now select the text you want to amend and do the following:

Click here; in the list which launches, select a colour

Font effects

You can also use the following keyboard shortcuts:

Ctrl++   *Superscript*
Ctrl+=   *Subscript*

You can use the following font effects in Word Processor documents:

- Superscript – e.g. f$^{\text{ont effect}}$

- Subscript – e.g. f$_{\text{ont effect}}$

- ~~Strikethrough~~

- SMALL CAPS

- ALL CAPS

Applying font effects

First, select the relevant text. Pull down the Format dialog and click Font. Then carry out the following steps:

1   Apply one or more effects in the Effects section (Small caps and All caps are mutually exclusive, as are Subscript and Superscript)

Underlining is an effect which is frequently used – there are various kinds in Works 7. Click in the Underline field and make a choice.

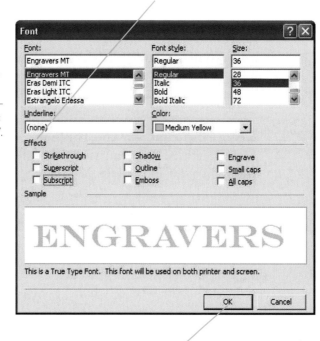

2   Click here

Using the Format Gallery

You can use a special feature known as the Format Gallery to apply fonts and colours (both arranged in collections known as 'sets') to your documents in a coordinated way. Formatting changes applied via the Format Gallery are mapped to underlying Works 7 templates, so the results are always harmonious. You can apply changes to specific text or the whole of the document.

Use Format Gallery with documents created via templates/ wizards rather than blank documents.

Applying formatting to specific text

1   Select the relevant text

2   Pull down the Format menu and select Format Gallery

3   Select the Format Item tab then select a font set in the list

4   Click here and select a colour set in the list

You can add your own formatting to the Gallery. Just select the relevant text then click the Add button.

To apply your formatting to selected text, just click its entry at the base of the Gallery.

5   Select an overall format (it will include the choices made in steps 4–5)

You can keep the Format Gallery onscreen as just a title bar and then make it appear when you need it – just click the chevron at the base of the Gallery.

6   If you don't like the results, repeat steps 4–5 until you do

By applying Format Gallery formatting to entire documents, you can save yourself a lot of time and effort:

- you won't need to format individual items separately

- you can be sure the results work well together

Applying formatting to a whole document

1 Pull down the Format menu and select Format Gallery

2 Select the Format All tab

3 Drag the slider to select a font set

4 Drag the slider to select a colour set

5 When you find a combination you like, click Apply All (or click Undo All if you want to discard your changes)

Indenting – an overview

Indents are a crucial component of document layout. For instance, in most document types indenting the first line of paragraphs (i.e. moving it inwards away from the left page margin) makes the text much more legible.

Other document types – e.g. bibliographies – can use the following:

You can achieve a similar effect by using tabs. However, indents are easier to apply (and amend subsequently).

- hanging indents (where the first line is unaltered, while subsequent lines are indented)

- full indents (where the entire paragraph is indented away from the left and/or the right margins)

Some of the potential indent combinations are shown in the illustration below:

Don't confuse indents with page margins. Margins are the gap between the edge of the page and the text area; indents define the distance between the margins and text.

The Word Processor doesn't actually display margins: they've been inserted here for illustration purposes.

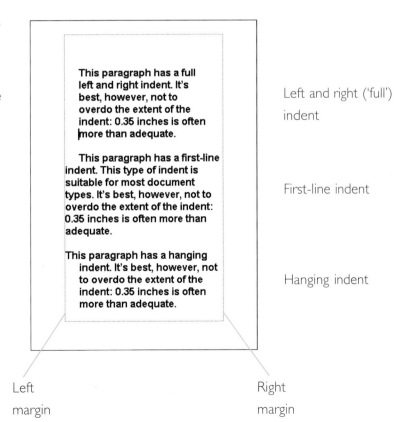

This paragraph has a full left and right indent. It's best, however, not to overdo the extent of the indent: 0.35 inches is often more than adequate.

Left and right ('full') indent

This paragraph has a first-line indent. This type of indent is suitable for most document types. It's best, however, not to overdo the extent of the indent: 0.35 inches is often more than adequate.

First-line indent

This paragraph has a hanging indent. It's best, however, not to overdo the extent of the indent: 0.35 inches is often more than adequate.

Hanging indent

Left margin

Right margin

Applying indents to paragraphs

Paragraphs can be indented from within the Paragraph dialog, or (to a lesser extent) by using the Formatting toolbar (if you add extra buttons to it).

Indenting text with the Font dialog

First, select the paragraph(s) you want to indent. Pull down the Format menu and click Paragraph. Now follow step 1 below. If you want a left indent, carry out step 2. For a right indent, follow step 3. To achieve a first-line or hanging indent, follow step 4. Finally, irrespective of the indent type, carry out step 5.

Ensure this tab is active

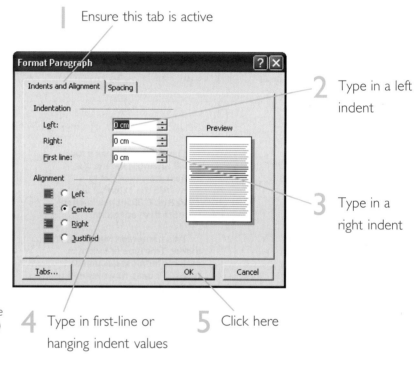

2 Type in a left indent

3 Type in a right indent

Re step 4 – to implement a hanging indent, type in a negative value (e.g. –0.35) and the equivalent value in the Left field (e.g. –0.35).

4 Type in first-line or hanging indent values

5 Click here

Using the Formatting toolbar to apply indents

Use these buttons in the Formatting toolbar:

 Moves the indent out one level

 Moves the indent in one level

Aligning paragraphs

You can use the following types of alignment:

Left   Text is flush with the left page margin

Center   Text aligns equidistantly between the left
                        and right page margins

Right   Text is flush with the right page margin

Justified   Text is flush with the left *and* right page
                        margins

Aligning text with the Format Paragraph dialog

First, select the paragraph(s) you want to align. Pull down the
Format menu and click Paragraph. Now:

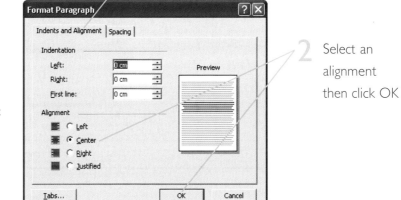

Ensure this tab is active

Select an alignment then click OK

*Justify can
sometimes
make text look
unattractive –
see the tip on
page 29.*

Aligning text with the Formatting toolbar

Select the relevant paragraph(s). Then refer to the Formatting
toolbar and click any of these buttons:

Left Align   Right Align

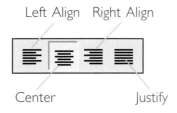

Center   Justify

Specifying paragraph spacing

You can customise the vertical space before and/or after specific text paragraphs. The Word Processor defines paragraph spacing in terms of whole lines.

As a general rule, set low paragraph spacing settings: a little goes a long way.

Applying paragraph spacing

1 Select the paragraph(s) whose spacing you want to adjust

2 Pull down the Format menu and select Paragraph

3 Ensure the Spacing tab is active

It's also often necessary to amend line spacing (also known as 'leading' – pronounced 'ledding'). This is the vertical distance between individual lines of text.

Click in the Line Spacing field and make a choice. Or use the following keystroke combinations:

Ctrl+1   Single spacing
Ctrl+5   1 ½ spacing
Ctrl+2   Double spacing
Ctrl+3   Triple spacing

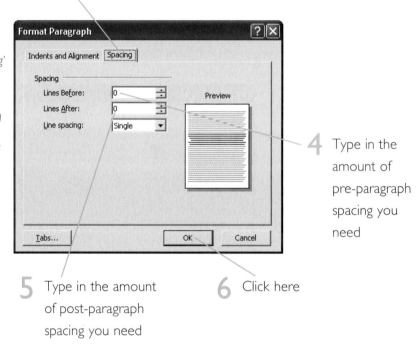

4 Type in the amount of pre-paragraph spacing you need

5 Type in the amount of post-paragraph spacing you need

6 Click here

Spacing and new documents
If you've just created a new document, you can set the paragraph spacing and/or line spacing before you begin to enter text.

Simply leave the insertion point at the start of the document and then follow the procedures outlined above.

Working with columns

The Word Processor module lets you arrange text into columns. You can:

- insert multiple columns (as many as 45)

- specify the inter-column gap

- have Works insert a vertical line between columns

Works 7 columns have certain restrictions. They apply to the entire document (not specific pages), and they have the same width (calculated automatically according to the left/right page margins and the inter-column gap).

Applying columns

1 Place the insertion point anywhere within the current Word Processor document

2 Pull down the Format menu and click Columns

3 Type in the no. of columns (depending on your margin settings and the inter-column gap)

If you want the columns separated by lines, select Line between columns.

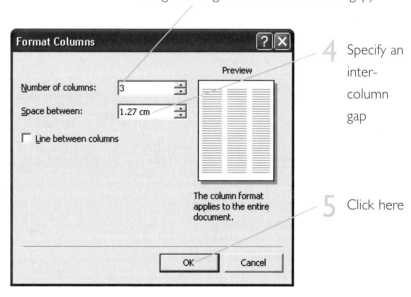

4 Specify an inter-column gap

5 Click here

Paragraph borders

By default, The Word Processor does not border paragraph text. However, you can apply a wide selection of borders if you want. You can specify:

• the border type/thickness

• how many sides the border should have (all four, or permutations of Left, Right, Top and Bottom)

• the border colour

Applying a border

First, select the paragraph(s) you want to border. Then pull down the Format menu and click Borders and Shading. Now do the following:

Ensure Paragraph is selected
then select a border style

Re step 2 – by default, Outline is selected. This means that all 4 sides are bordered. If you don't want this, deselect Outline then select one or more individual options (e.g. Left, or Top and Right).

You can also apply a fill to selected paragraphs. Click in the Fill Style field to select a fill type. Then click in the Color 1 field to select a shading colour, and/or in the Color 2 field to select a line/dot colour.

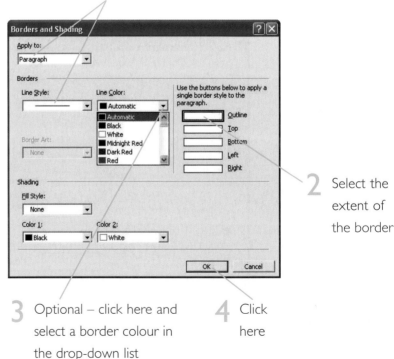

2 Select the extent of the border

3 Optional – click here and select a border colour in the drop-down list

4 Click here

Working with tabs

Tabs are a means of indenting the first line of text paragraphs (you can also use indents for this purpose – see pages 37–38).

When you press the Tab key while the text insertion point is at the start of a paragraph, the text in the first line jumps to the next tab stop:

The gap before the 'Lorem' is a tab in action – for how to view the underlying tab mark, see page 28.

Theme 1/1/2000

> *Lorem ipsum dolor sit amet, consectetuer adipiscing elit, sed diam nonummy nibh euismod tincidunt ut laoreet dolore magna aliquam erat volutpat. Ut wisi enim ad minim veniam, quis nostrud exercitation ullamcorper suscipit lobortis nisl ut aliquip ex ea commodo consequat. Duis te feugifacilisi. Duis autem dolor in hendrerit in vulputate velit esse.*

This is a useful way to increase the legibility of your text.

By default, tab stops are inserted automatically every half an inch. If you want, however, you can enter new or revised tab stop positions individually.

Never use the Space Bar to indent paragraphs. The result is uneven, because spaces vary in size according to the typeface and type size applying to specific paragraphs.

Setting tab stops

First, select the paragraph(s) in which you need to set tab stops. Pull down the Format menu and do the following:

Click here

2 If existing individual tab stops are present (see the tip), carry out step 4 below

3 If you want to implement a new default tab stop position, follow step 5. If, on the other hand, you need to set up individual tab stops, carry out steps 6–7 as often as necessary. Finally, in either case follow step 8 to confirm your changes

6 Type in a single tab stop

7 Click here

When you've performed steps 6–7, the individual tab stop position appears in the Tab stops box.

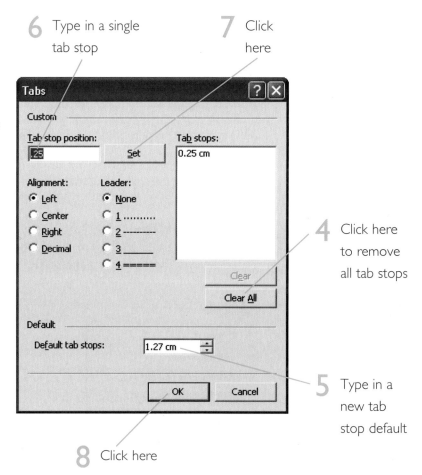

4 Click here to remove all tab stops

5 Type in a new tab stop default

8 Click here

Searching for text

You can search for specific text within the active document.

You can also search for special characters. For example, you can look for paragraph marks, tabs, wildcards, question marks, page breaks and spaces.

You can also:

- limit the search to words which match the case of the text you specify (e.g. if you search for 'Arm', Works 7 will not flag 'arm' or 'ARM') – see step 2

- limit the search to whole words (e.g. if you search for 'eat', Works will not flag 'beat' or 'meat') – see step 2

Initiating a text search

Pull down the Edit menu and click Find (or just press Ctrl+F). Carry out step 1. Perform steps 2 and 3–4 as appropriate. Finally, carry out step 5:

Type in the text you want to find

Find and Replace

Find | Replace | Go to

Find what: Christmas Bonus

☐ Match case
☐ Find whole words only

Special ▾

Find Next   Cancel

3 Click here

5 Click here

There are three wildcards (characters which can stand for others). These are:

Any Digit — *Stands for any number*

Any Letter — *Stands for any letter*

Any Character — *Stands for any number or letter*

Select any of these in step 4.

2 Activate one or both of these

4 Select a character

Paragraph Mark
Tab Character
Any Character
Any Digit
Any Letter
Caret Character
Nonbreaking Hyphen
Nonbreaking Space
White Space

Replacing text

When you've located text, you can have the Word Processor replace it automatically with the text of your choice.

You can customise find-and-replace operations with the same parameters as a simple Find operation. For example, you can make them case-specific, or only replace whole words. You can also incorporate a variety of special characters.

Initiating a find-and-replace operation

First pull down the Edit menu and click Replace (or press Ctrl+H). Follow step 1 and/or steps 4–5 (if appropriate). Carry out step 2 and/or steps 4–5 (if relevant). Perform step 3, if applicable. Finally, perform step 6 (or see the DON'T FORGET tip):

Re steps 4–5 – if you launch the special character menu after step 2, fewer options display. (For obvious reasons, wildcards are unavailable.)

If you don't want all instances of the text replaced automatically, don't carry out step 6. Instead, click the Find Next button after step 5. When the first match has been found, do one of the following:

- *click Replace if you want it replaced, or;*
- *click Find Next again to leave it alone and locate the next match*

Repeat this as often as necessary.

1 Type in the text you want to find

2 Type in the replacement text

4 Click here

6 Click Replace All

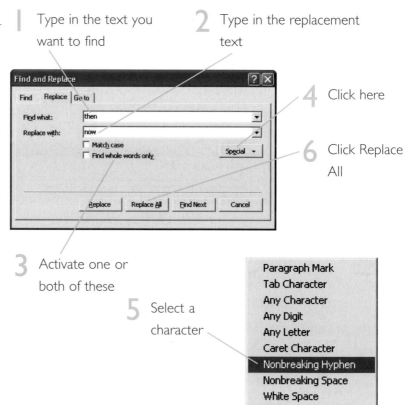

3 Activate one or both of these

5 Select a character

Paragraph Mark
Tab Character
Any Character
Any Digit
Any Letter
Caret Character
Nonbreaking Hyphen
Nonbreaking Space
White Space

Inserting headers

You can have the Word Processor print text at the top of each page within a document; the area of the page where repeated text appears is called the 'header'. In the same way, you can have text printed at the base of each page; in this case, the relevant page area is called the 'footer'. Headers and footers are printed within the top and bottom page margins, respectively.

By default, the header and footer areas (but not the contents) are invisible.

To amend a header, follow steps 1–3. In step 2, edit it as necessary.

Re step 2 – to insert a special code which automatically inserts the page number in the header, click this button in the Header/Footer toolbar:

Creating a header

1   Pull down the View menu and click Header and Footer

2   Enter – then format –   The Header/
    the relevant header text   Footer toolbar

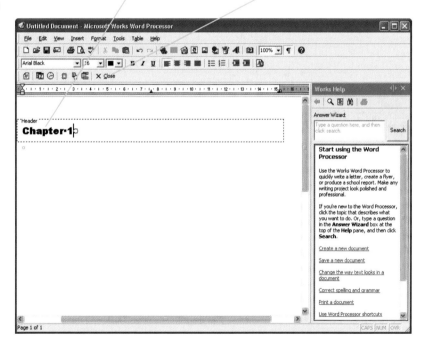

3   When you've finished, click Close in the dedicated toolbar

Inserting footers

Creating a footer

To amend a footer, follow steps 1–4. In step 3, edit it as necessary.

1 Pull down the View menu and click Header and Footer

2 Click this button in the Header/Footer toolbar:

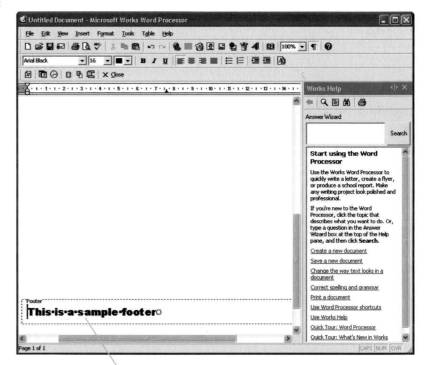

You can insert a special code which automatically inserts the page number in the footer. See the Don't Forget tip on page 47.

3 Enter – then format – the relevant footer text

4 When you've finished, click Close in the dedicated toolbar

Undoing actions

The Word Processor lets you reverse – 'undo' – just about any editing operation.

You can undo up to 100 consecutive actions in the following ways (in descending order of complexity):

- via the keyboard

- from within the Edit menu

- from within the Standard toolbar

To undo an undo (i.e. redo the action you reversed), press Ctrl+Y instead.

Using the keyboard
Simply press Ctrl+Z to undo an action. Repeat to perform consecutive undos.

Using the Edit menu
Pull down the Edit menu and do the following:

To undo an undo, click Redo... instead.

Click Undo ... (where the ellipses represent the most recent editing action)

Using the Standard toolbar
Refer to the Standard toolbar and do the following:

To undo an undo, click the button to the right of the Undo button.

Click here (repeat if necessary)

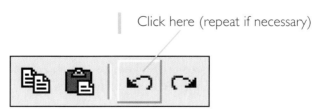

Spell-checking

You can check text in two ways:

- on-the-fly, as you type in text

- separately, after the text has been entered

Checking text on-the-fly

This is the default. When automatic checking is in force, Works 7 flags words it doesn't agree with, using a wavy red underline. If the word or phrase is wrong, right-click in it. Then carry out steps 1, 2 or 3:

> Works 7 often provides a list of alternatives. If one is correct, click it; the flagged word is replaced with the correct version

Re step 2 – when Works has flagged a word you have an extra option. Click Add if the flagged word is correct and you want Works to remember it in future spell-checks (by adding it to your personal dictionary – see the DON'T FORGET tip on the facing page).

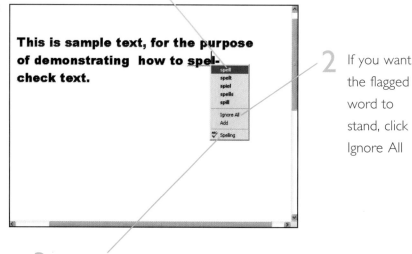

This is sample text, for the purpose of demonstrating how to spell-check text.

2 If you want the flagged word to stand, click Ignore All

3 If the flagged word is wrong but can't be corrected now, click Spelling and complete the resulting dialog – see the facing page

Disabling on-the-fly spell-checking

On-the-fly checking can sometimes become a nuisance. To turn it off, pull down the Tools menu and click Options. Deselect Background spell checking. Click OK.

...cont'd

Checking text separately

To check all the text within the active document in one go, pull down the Tools menu and click Spelling and Grammar. The Word Processor starts spell-checking the document from the text insertion point. When it encounters a word or phrase it doesn't recognise, Works 7 flags it and produces a special dialog (see below). Usually, it provides alternative suggestions; if one of these is correct, you can opt to have it replace the flagged word. You can do this singly (i.e. just this instance is replaced) or globally (where all future instances – within the current checking session – are replaced).

Alternatively, you can have Works ignore *this* instance of the flagged word, ignore *all* future instances of the word or add the word to your personal dictionary (see the tips). After this, checking is resumed.

Carry out step 1 below, then follow step 2. Alternatively, carry out step 3 or 4 (or see the HOT TIP).

Works 7 makes use of two separate dictionaries. One – called your personal dictionary – is yours. When you click the Add button (see the tip below and on the facing page), the flagged word is stored in your personal dictionary and recognised in future checking sessions.

If you're correcting a spelling error, you have two further options:

- *click Add to have the flagged word stored in your personal dictionary (see above), or;*
- *click Change All to have Works substitute its suggestion for all future instances of the flagged word*

If one of the suggestions here is correct, click it, then follow step 2

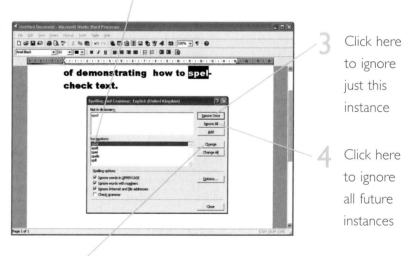

3 Click here to ignore just this instance

4 Click here to ignore all future instances

2 Click here to replace this instance

Grammar-checking

You can also have the Word Processor check a document's grammar (but only as a separate operation, not on-the-fly). It does this by applying collections of rules called 'writing styles'. There are two writing styles you can choose from:

- Grammar Only

- Grammar & Style

Grammar-checking text

Pull down the Tools menu and click Spelling and Grammar. Carry out step 1 below, then follow step 2. Alternatively, carry out step 3 or 4.

To apply a new writing style, launch the Spelling and Grammar dialog. Now click the Options button. In the Options dialog, click in the Writing style: field. In the list, click a style. Click OK, then resume grammar-checking.

To disable grammar-checking (so that only spelling mistakes are flagged), launch the Options dialog (see the above tip). In the dialog, deselect Check grammar. Click OK.

If you aren't sure about the grammatical rule currently being exercised, click the Explain Rule button for clarification.

1 If a suggestion is correct, click it then follow step 2

3 Click Ignore Once to ignore just this instance

4 Click Ignore Rule to ignore all future instances in this session

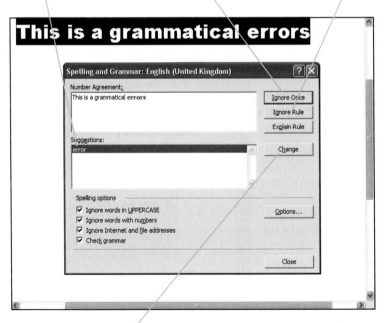

2 Click Change to replace this instance

Searching for synonyms

You can search for synonyms while you're editing the active document. You do this by calling up the resident Thesaurus. The Thesaurus categorises words into meanings, and each meaning is allocated various synonyms from which you can choose.

As a bonus, the Thesaurus also supplies:

- antonyms (e.g. if you look up 'good', Works lists 'poor')

- related words (e.g. if you look up 'author', Works lists 'critic')

Using the Thesaurus

First, select the word for which you require a synonym, antonym or related term. (Or simply position the insertion point within it). Pull down the Tools menu and click Thesaurus (or simply press Shift+F7). Now do the following:

1 The selected word appears here

3 Click Replace to substitute the replacement word

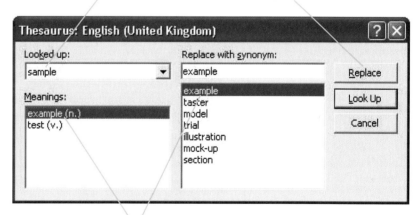

2 Select a meaning then click a replacement word

Working with images

The Word Processor module lets you add colour or greyscale images to the active document. Images – also called graphics – include:

- drawings produced in other programs

- clip art

- scanned photographs

Use images – whatever their source – to add much needed visual impact to documents. But use them judiciously: too much colour can be off-putting, and ultimately self-defeating.

Images are stored in various third-party formats. These formats are organised into two basic types:

Bitmap images

Bitmaps consist of pixels (dots) arranged in such a way that they form a graphic image. Because of the very nature of bitmaps, the question of 'resolution' – the sharpness of an image expressed in dpi (dots per inch) – is very important. Bitmaps look best if they're displayed at their native resolution. Works 7 can manipulate a wide variety of third-party bitmap graphics formats. These include: PCX, TIF and GIF.

Vector images

You can also insert vector graphics files into Word Processor documents. Vector images consist of and are defined by algebraic equations. They're less complex than bitmaps: they contain less detail. Vector files can also include bitmap information.

Irrespective of the format type, Works can incorporate images with the help of special 'filters'. These are special mini-programs whose job it is to translate third-party formats into a form which Works can use.

Brief notes on image formats

Works 7 will happily import a wide selection of bitmap and vector graphic formats. These are some of the main formats:

Bitmap formats

The main supported vector format is Windows Metafile (suffix .WMF).

This format is used for information exchange between just about all Windows programs, and often produces files which are much smaller than the equivalent bitmaps (though not because of compression – there isn't any).

BMP   Not as common as PCX and TIFF, but still popular. One drawback: sometimes, compression isn't normally available.

GIF   Graphics Interchange Format. Developed for the online transmission of graphics data across the CompuServe network. Just about any Windows program – and a lot more besides – will read GIF. Disadvantage: it can't handle more than 256 colours. One of the few graphics formats which can be used in HTML (HyperText Markup Language) documents on the World Wide Web. Compression is supported.

JPEG   Joint Photographic Experts Group. Suffix: .JPG. Used on the PC and Mac for the storage and display of photographs. One of the few graphics formats which can be used in HTML (HyperText Markup Language) documents on the World Wide Web. A very high level of compression is built into the format.

PCD   (Kodak) PhotoCD. Used primarily to store photographs on CD.

PCX   An old standby. Originated with PC Paintbrush, a paint program. Used for years to transfer graphics data between Windows applications. Supports compression.

PNG   Portable Network Graphics. Supports high compression, making it very handy for use on the Web, but unfortunately is still not supported by all browsers.

TIFF   Tagged Image File Format. Suffix: .TIF. If anything, even more widely used than PCX, across a whole range of platforms and applications. Supports numerous types and levels of compression.

Inserting graphics

Works 7 lets you insert clip art and pictures into your Word Processor documents. By clip art, Works means the image files supplied on the program CD. The term 'pictures', on the other hand, refers to third-party graphics formats (e.g. TIFF and PCX).

You add clip art with the use of a special dialog.

Inserting clip art

1   Make sure your Works 7 CD is in its drive

2   Within the relevant Word Processor document, click where you want the clip art inserted

3   Pull down the Insert menu and click Picture, Clip Art

4   Select a category   6   Select a clip

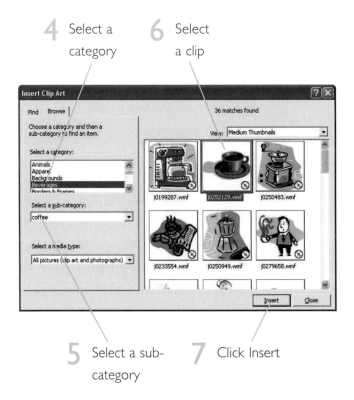

5   Select a sub-category   7   Click Insert

Inserting third-party pictures

1 If appropriate, make sure the source CD is in the drive

2 Within the relevant Word Processor document, click where you want the picture inserted

3 Pull down the Insert menu and click Picture, From File

4 Select a drive

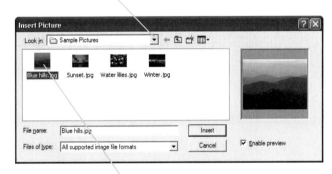

5 Double-click a picture

The inserted picture

Searching for keywords

The clip art images supplied with Works 7 have keywords associated with them (this means that, if you want to find a specific picture, you can run a keyword search).

To search for clip art by one or more keywords, do the following:

1 Pull down the Insert menu and click Picture, Clip Art

2 Ensure the Find tab is active then type in one or more keywords (or a key phrase)

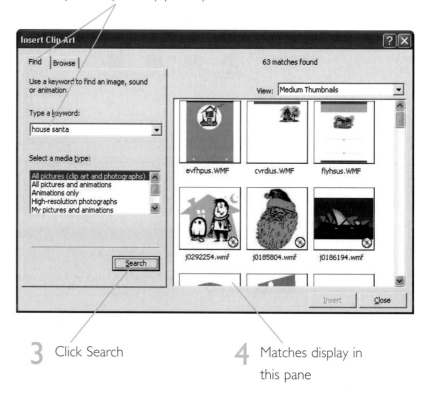

3 Click Search

4 Matches display in this pane

Inserting tables

You can also insert spreadsheets into Word Processor documents (giving you more spreadsheet functionality in situ).

Pull down the Insert menu and click Spreadsheet. The Spreadsheet module takes over the Word Processor menus and toolbars, so you are in effect working with the Spreadsheet module in the Word Processor.

You can easily insert tables into your Word Processor documents. Tables are highly customisable and make data visually attractive. If you want to work with lots of data, use tables rather than creating columns by inserting tab stops.

Inserting a table

1 Pull down the Table menu and click Insert Table

2 Select a format

3 Complete the 4 fields here

Tables work like spreadsheets. Click in 'cells' to edit them. Press Tab or Shift+Tab to move from cell to cell. To edit row or column structure, or the table format, right-click in a row or column and make the appropriate menu choice.

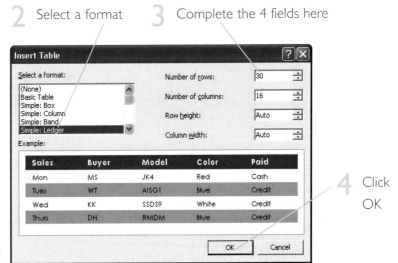

4 Click OK

5 Start to enter data

Inserting watermarks

Watermarks are pictures inserted into other images as faint backgrounds. Adding watermarks to your pictures can create an appealing and effective impact.

Adding watermarks

1 Pull down the Insert menu and click Watermark

2 Select Picture watermark

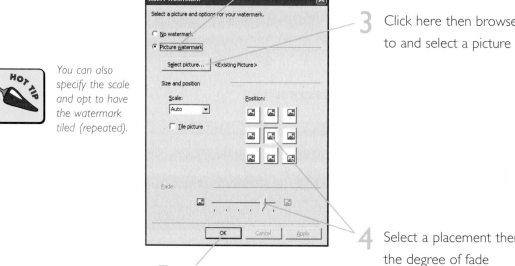

You can also specify the scale and opt to have the watermark tiled (repeated).

3 Click here then browse to and select a picture

4 Select a placement then the degree of fade

5 Click here

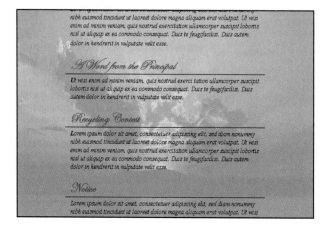

An inserted watermark

Rescaling images

There are two ways in which you can rescale images:

- proportionally, where the height/width ratio remains constant

- disproportionately, where the height/width ratio is disrupted (this is sometimes called 'warping' or 'skewing')

1 Select the image

You can also use a special dialog to rescale images – see overleaf.

2 Move the mouse pointer over one of the corner handles (if you want to rescale the image proportionally) or one of the handles in the middle of the sides (if you want to warp it)

3 Drag outwards to increase the image size or inwards to decrease it

Here, the image from page 57 has been skewed from the right inwards

Rescaling images – the dialog route

You can use a special dialog to rescale images, a method which allows much greater precision (though it does take longer).

1 Select the image

2 Pull down the Format menu and click Object

3 Ensure the Size tab is active   4 Enter new width & height measurements

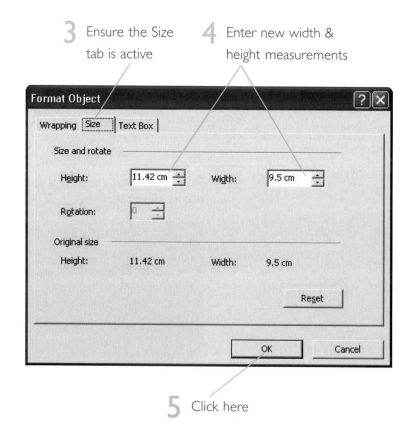

5 Click here

Moving images

You can easily move images from one place on the page to another.

First, click the image to select it. Move the mouse pointer over it; it changes to a pointing arrow. Left-click once and hold down the button. Drag the image to its new location.

Move cursor

Release the mouse button to confirm the move.

Problems with Move operations?

If dragging has no effect, this is probably because the 'In line with text' text wrap option is in force (Works 7 is treating the graphic as part of the paragraph). Do the following to correct this situation:

1 Select the graphic

2 Apply Square or Tight text wrap to it (see page 66)

3 Repeat the Move operation

Wrapping text around images

If you insert clip art or pictures into documents which contain text, it's often useful to have the text flow ('wrap') around the graphics rather than through them. There are various options.

Text wrap options

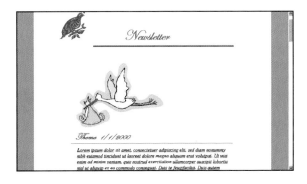

In line with text (no text to the side)

Square (the image is bounded by an imaginary box and the text wraps round this)

Tight (the text contours around the image's shape)

Applying text wrap

1 Select the image

2 Pull down the Format menu and click Object

3 Ensure the Wrapping
  tab is active

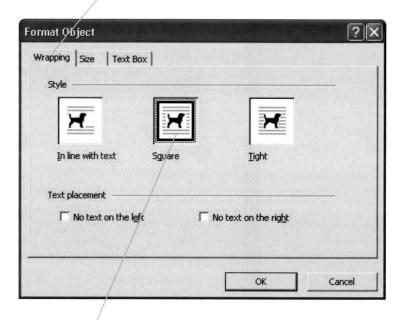

4 Select a wrap type

5 If you selected Square or Tight in step 4, you can disable text
  wrap for the left or right side of the image. Simply select No text
  on the left, or No text on the right

6 Click OK when you've finished

Carrying out mail merges

You can use the Word Processor Mail Merge facility to automatically address letters. Mail Merge gets its information from the Works Address Book – this is then added to your document (known as the 'merge document'). Using Mail Merge is a great timesaver.

You can save your merge document in the normal way.

The merge document contains each copy of the individually addressed letters, and you can view these at will before printing.

Creating a merge document

1 Run the Task Launcher in the usual way

2 Select Tasks then Letters & Labels

3 Select Letters then Start this task

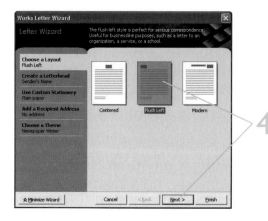

4 Select a style and click Next

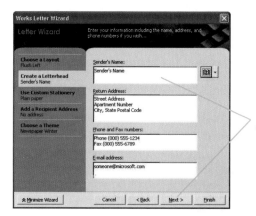

5 Complete sender information and select Next

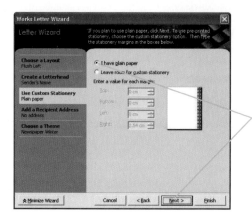

6 Unless you're using pre-printed stationery, select I have plain paper and click Next

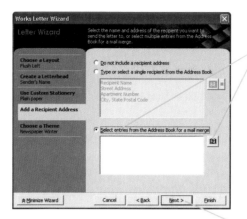

7 Select this option then click the book icon. To include a contact, select it in the Address Book then click Select. Repeat as necessary then click OK

8 Click Next

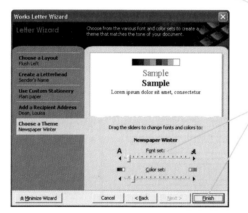

9 As in the Format Gallery, select the font/colour set you want then click Finish

After step 9, Works enters the first set of contact details into the merge document. To see more contacts, click the right-pointing arrow in the View Results window.

To print your letter (i.e. one copy prints for each included Address Book contact), press Ctrl+P. Complete the Print dialog as usual (but also complete the Mail Merge Print Settings section). Select OK to print.

The merge document showing the details for the 1st contact

Page setup – an overview

You can control the following aspects of page layout in the Word Processor module:

- the top, bottom, left and/or right page margins

- the distance between the top page edge and the top edge of the header

- the distance between the bottom page edge and bottom edge of the footer

The illustration below shows these page components:

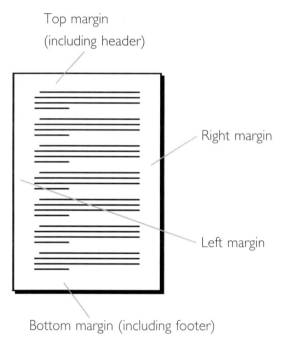

Top margin
(including header)

Right margin

Left margin

Bottom margin (including footer)

You can also specify:

- the overall page size (inclusive of margins and headers/ footers)

- the page orientation ('landscape' or 'portrait')

If none of the supplied page sizes is suitable, you can even customise your own.

Specifying margins

Margin settings are the framework on which indents and tabs are based.

All documents have margins, because printing on the whole of a sheet is both unsightly and – in the case of many printers, since the mechanism has to grip the page – impossible. Documents need a certain amount of 'white space' (the unprinted portion of the page) to balance the areas which contain text and graphics. Without this, they can't be visually effective.

As a result, it's important to set margins correctly. Fortunately, the Word Processor module makes the job of changing margin settings easy. Note, however, that you can only adjust margin settings on a document-wide basis (i.e. not for individual pages).

Customising margins

1 Pull down the File menu and click Page Setup

2 Ensure the Margins tab is active then enter new margin settings in any of these fields

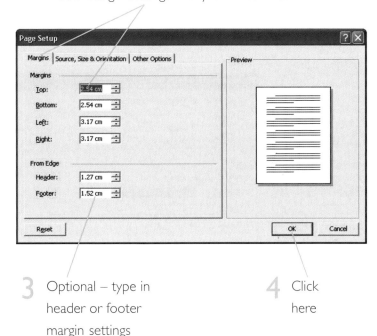

3 Optional – type in header or footer margin settings

4 Click here

Specifying the page size

The Word Processor comes with numerous preset page sizes. These are suitable for most purposes. However, if you need to you can also set up your own page definition.

There are two aspects to every page size:

• a vertical measurement

• a horizontal measurement

There are two possible orientations: Portrait, where the vertical measurement is the longest, and Landscape where the reverse applies.

Setting the page size
Pull down the File menu and do the following:

1 Pull down the File menu and click Page Setup

2 Ensure the Source, Size & Orientation tab is active

3 Select an orientation

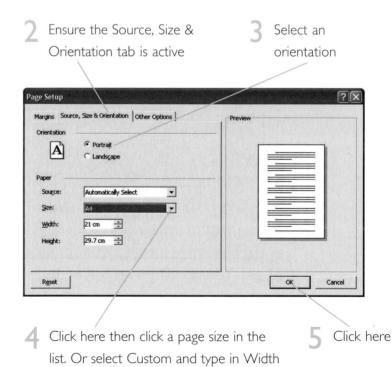

4 Click here then click a page size in the list. Or select Custom and type in Width and Height settings to create your own

5 Click here

Using Print Preview

The Word Processor provides a special view mode called Print Preview. This displays the active document exactly as it will look when printed.

Use Print Preview as a final check just before you print your document.

Although you can't specify the precise number of pages displayed, you can specify:

- *One Page*
- *Two Pages*
- *Multiple Pages (the Word Processor displays as many full pages as possible)*

When you're using Print Preview, you can zoom in or out on the active page. What you can't do, however, is specify the number of pages displayed or edit or revise the active document.

Launching Print Preview

Pull down the File menu and click Print Preview. This is the result:

If the Print Preview command is greyed out and therefore unavailable, check that your printer is connected properly, and its driver is installed and working.

Click Close (or press Esc) to leave Print Preview

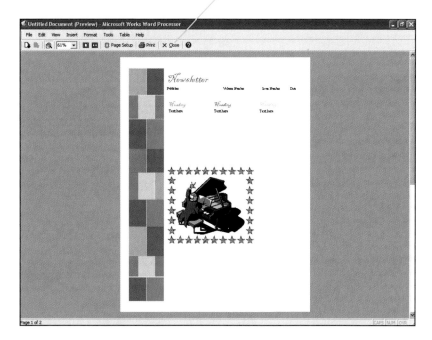

Zooming in or out in Print Preview

There are two methods you can use here.

Using the mouse
Do the following:

Move the mouse pointer over the page (it changes to a magnifying glass)

Clicking again with the magnifying glass cursor returns the magnification to the original level.

2 Left-click once to increase the magnification. If this doesn't work, click this toolbar button and repeat:

Using the Print Preview toolbar
Launch Print Preview. Then carry out the following actions:

Type in a Zoom percentage (in the range 25–500%) and press Enter. (Or click the arrow and select a preset level)

Changing pages in Print Preview

In Print Preview, you can also step backwards and forwards through the active document as often as necessary.

There are three methods you can use (in descending order of usefulness).

Using the dedicated toolbar
Carry out the following actions:

Depending on your location within the document (and the number of pages), one of these buttons may be greyed out, and therefore unavailable.

Click here to jump to the next page

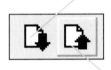

Click here to jump to the previous page

Using the keyboard
You can use the following keyboard shortcuts:

Page Up — Moves to the previous page (within a magnified page view, moves through the current page instead)

Page Down — Moves to the next page (within a magnified page view, moves through the current page instead)

Using the scrollbars
When you're working with a magnified view of a page, use the vertical and/or horizontal scrollbars (using standard Windows techniques) to move up or down within the page.

Printer setup

Most Word Processor documents need to be printed eventually. Before you can begin printing, however, you must ensure that:

- the correct printer is selected (if you have more than one installed)

- the correct printer settings are in force

Works 7 calls these collectively the 'printer setup'.

Irrespective of the printer selected, the settings vary in accordance with the job in hand. For example, most printer drivers (the software which 'drives' the printer) allow you to specify whether or not you want pictures printed. Additionally, they often allow you to specify the resolution or print quality of the output.

Selecting the printer and/or settings

Just before you're ready to print a document, pull down the File menu and click Print. Now do the following:

The question of which printer you select affects how the document displays in Print Preview mode.

Click here; select the printer you want from the list

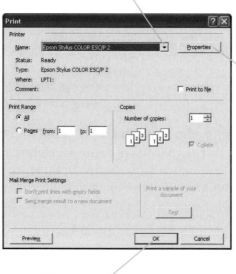

2 Click here to adjust the printer settings (then complete the dialog which launches) – see your printer's manual for details

Set any print options which are required before carrying out step 3.

3 Click here to begin printing

Customised printing

If you need to set revised print options before printing, pull down the File menu and click Print. Now carry out steps 1–3 below, as appropriate. To inspect your document in Print Preview mode before printing, follow steps 4–5. Finally (if you haven't performed steps 4–5) carry out step 6 to begin printing.

To print to a file instead of a printer, customise your print job in the usual way. Then select Print to file and carry out step 6. The Print to file dialog appears. Select a drive/ folder combination for the new file, then name it. Click OK. The Word Processor now saves your print job as a file.

Collation is the process whereby Works prints one full copy at a time. For instance, if you're printing three copies of a 40-page document, Works prints pages 1–40 of the first document, followed by pages 1–40 of the second and pages 1–40 of the third.

3 Type in start and end pages

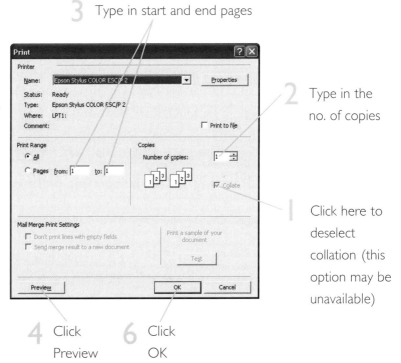

2 Type in the no. of copies

Click here to deselect collation (this option may be unavailable)

4 Click Preview   6 Click OK

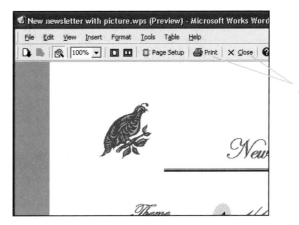

5 Click Close to close Preview without printing or Print to print the document immediately

Printing – the fast track approach

There are occasions when you'll merely want to print out your work:

- bypassing the Print dialog

- with the current settings applying

- with a single mouse click

One reason for this is proofing. Irrespective of how rigorously you check documents onscreen, there will always be errors and deficiencies which, with the best will in the world, will be difficult or impossible to pick up. By initiating printing with the minimum of delay, you can check your work much more rapidly...

For this reason, Works 7 provides a printing method which is especially quick and easy to use.

Printing with the current print options

1 Ensure your printer is ready, and your document is ready to print

2 Make sure the Standard toolbar is visible. (If it isn't, pull down the View menu and click Toolbars, Standard)

3 Click here

4 Printing begins immediately

Spreadsheet

This chapter shows you how to carry out basic/advanced data editing in the Spreadsheet module. You'll learn how to work with data and formulas, and how to move around in spreadsheets. You'll also discover how to locate data, and make it more visually effective by converting it to charts. Finally, you'll customise page layout/printing.

Covers

Chapter Three

The Spreadsheet screen

Below is a detailed illustration of the Spreadsheet screen:

Menu bar   Title bar   Entry bar   Column headings

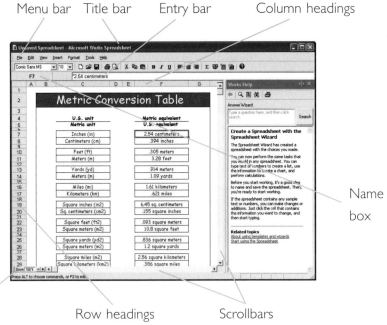

Name box

Row headings   Scrollbars

This is the Zoom Area: The screen components here are used to adjust magnification levels. See pages 88–89.

Some of these – e.g. the scrollbars – are standard to just about all programs which run under Windows. One – the Toolbar – can be hidden, if required.

Specifying whether the Toolbar displays

Pull down the View menu and select Toolbar. Then:

Click Use Large Icons if you want bigger buttons in the Toolbar.

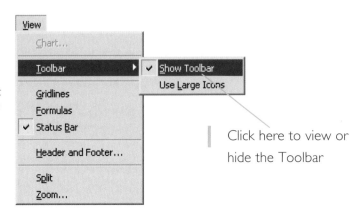

Click here to view or hide the Toolbar

Entering data

Columns are vertical, rows horizontal. Each spreadsheet can have as many as 256 columns and 16,384 rows, making a grand total of 4,194,304 cells.

When you start the Works 7 Spreadsheet module, you can use the Task Launcher to create a new blank spreadsheet (see Chapter 1 for how to do this). This excerpt is typical of the result:

	A	B	C
1			
2			
3			
4			
5			
6			
7			
8			
9			
10			
11			
12			

Cells

This means that you can start entering data immediately.

In the Spreadsheet module, you can enter the following basic data types:

- values (i.e. numbers)

- text (e.g. headings and explanatory material)

- functions (e.g. Sine or Cosine)

- formulas (combinations of values, text and functions)

You enter data into 'cells'. Cells are formed where rows and columns intersect. In the most basic sense, collections of rows/ columns and cells are known as spreadsheets.

In-cell editing may be disabled. To restore it, pull down the Tools menu and click Options. In the Options dialog, select the Data Entry tab and tick In cells and the formula bar. Click OK.

Although you can enter data *directly* into a cell (by clicking in it, typing it in and pressing Enter), there's another method you can use which is often easier. The Spreadsheet provides a special screen component known as the Entry bar.

The illustration below shows the end of a blank spreadsheet. Some sample text has been inserted into cell IV16384 (currently off-screen). The Name box tells you which cell is currently active:

Name box

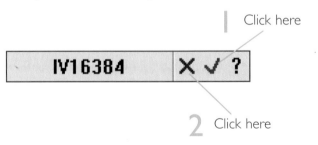

Entry bar

Entering data via the Entry bar

Click the cell you want to insert data into. Click the Entry bar. Type in the data. Then follow step 1 below. If you decide to cancel the operation, follow step 2 instead:

You can use a keyboard route to confirm operations in the Entry bar. Simply press Return. (Press Esc to cancel them.)

Click here

IV16384 X ✓ ?

2 Click here

Modifying existing data

You can spell-check spreadsheet contents. Press F7 and complete the dialog.

You can amend the contents of a cell in two ways:

* via the Entry bar

* from within the cell

When you use either of these methods, the Spreadsheet enters a special state known as Edit Mode.

Amending existing data using the Entry bar

Click the cell whose contents you want to change. Then click in the Entry bar. Make the appropriate revisions and/or additions. Then press Return. The relevant cell is updated.

To launch the Financial Worksheets Wizard, click Programs in the Task Launcher. Select Works Spreadsheet, Financial worksheets. Now click the Start this task button and follow the on-screen instructions.

Amending existing data internally

Click the cell whose contents you want to change. Press F2. Make the appropriate revisions and/or additions *within the cell*. Then press Return.

The illustration below shows a section of a spreadsheet created with the Financial Worksheets Wizard:

You can 'freeze' row/column titles so that they remain on screen when you move to other parts of the active spreadsheet.

Select the row below the row you want to freeze, or the column to the right of the column you want to freeze. Pull down the Format menu and click Freeze Titles.

To unfreeze all frozen titles, pull down the Format menu and deselect Freeze Titles.

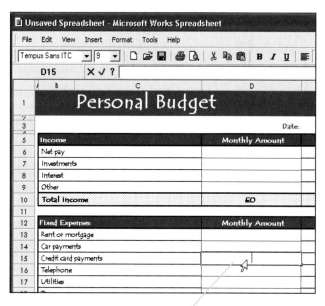

Cell D15 in Edit Mode

Sharing data with Excel 2002

In Works 7, you can 'round-trip' files to Microsoft Excel 2002, edit them there and then re-export them to Works 7.

Exporting to Excel 2002

1 Follow the procedures on page 18. Before step 3, however, click in the Save as type: field and select Excel 97-2000 (*.xls)

2 Open the Excel-format file in Excel 2002 itself

3 Make any desired editing changes then save them and close the file

Because Excel 2002 supports more features than Works 7, some of them will be lost if you import native Excel 2002 worksheets into Works. For example, comments are deleted and PivotTables are converted to straight data. Also, Excel charts have to be recreated in Works.

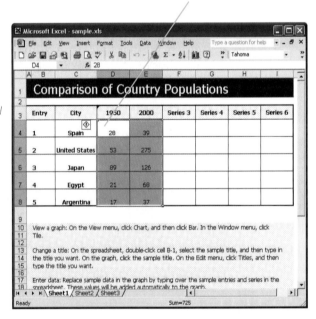

4 In the Works Spreadsheet module , press Ctrl+O. In the Files of type: field in the Open dialog, select Excel SS (*.xl*)

5 Locate then double-click the Excel spreadsheet to open it

6 In the Import Excel Spreadsheet dialog, select a spreadsheet (normally Sheet1) and click OK

Working with cell ranges

When you're working with more than one cell, it's often convenient and useful to organise them in 'ranges'.

A range is a rectangular arrangement of cells. In the illustration below, all cells between C10 and J19 have been selected.

Cells in a selected range are coloured black, with the exception of the first

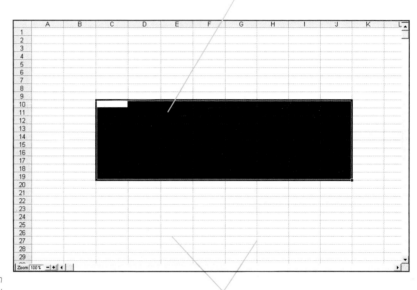

To hide gridlines (or to make them visible again), pull down the View menu and click Gridlines.

Gridlines (these make the underlying structure of a spreadsheet's component cells more visible)

You can name ranges, for even greater ease of use. To do this, select the range. Pull down the Insert menu and click Range Name. In the Name field in the Range Name dialog, type in a name. Click OK.

Cell 'shorthand'

The above description of the relevant cells is very cumbersome. It's much more useful to use a form of shorthand. The Spreadsheet module (using the start and end cells as reference points) refers to these cells as:

C10:J19

This notation system makes it much easier to refer to sizeable cell ranges.

Moving around in spreadsheets

Spreadsheets can be huge. Moving to cells which happen currently to be visible is easy: you simply click in the relevant cell. However, the Spreadsheet module provides several techniques you can use to jump to less accessible areas.

Using the scrollbars

Use any of the following methods:

1. To scroll quickly to another section of the active spreadsheet, drag the scroll box along the scrollbar until you reach it

2. To move one window to the left or right, click to the left or right of the scroll box in the horizontal scrollbar

3. To move one window up or down, click above or below the scroll box in the vertical scrollbar

4. To move up or down by one row, click the arrows in the vertical scrollbar

5. To move left or right by one column, click the arrows in the horizontal scrollbar

Scrollbar

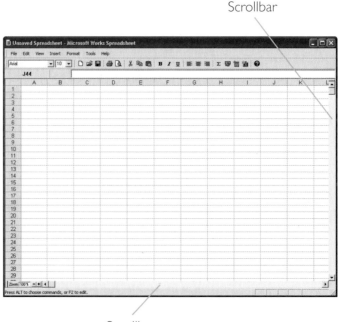

Scrollbar

Using the keyboard
You can use the following techniques:

1.   Use the cursor keys to move one cell left, right, up or down

2.   Hold down Ctrl as you use 1. above; this jumps to the edge of the current section (e.g. if cell B11 is active and you hold down Ctrl as you press →, Works 7 jumps to IV11, the last cell in row 11)

3.   Press Home to jump to the first cell in the active row, or Ctrl+Home to move to A1

4.   Press Page Up or Page Down to move up or down by one screen

5.   Press Ctrl+Page Down to move one screen to the right, or Ctrl+Page Up to move one screen to the left

Using the Go To dialog
Pull down the Edit menu and click Go To (or just press Ctrl+G). Now do the following:

1 Type in the cell reference you want to move to

2 Or select a print area here (see page 123)

Re step 1 – a cell's 'reference' (or 'address') identifies it in relation to its position in a spreadsheet, e.g. B11 or H23.

You can also type in cell ranges here (e.g. B11:C15), or range names.

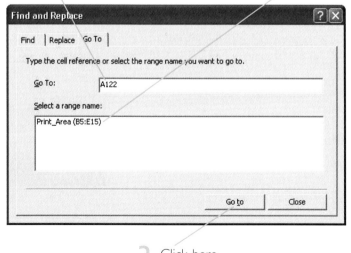

3 Click here

Changing zoom levels

The ability to vary the level of magnification for the active document is especially useful for spreadsheets, which very often occupy more space than can be accommodated on-screen at any given time. Sometimes, it's helpful to 'zoom out' (i.e. decrease the magnification) so that you can take an overview; at other times, you'll need to 'zoom in' (increase the magnification) to work in greater detail.

You can alter magnification levels in the Spreadsheet module:

- with the use of the Zoom Area

- with the Zoom dialog

Using the Zoom Area

You can use the Zoom Area (at the base of the screen) to alter zoom levels with the minimum of effort. Carry out step 1 OR 2, or steps 3 AND 4, as appropriate:

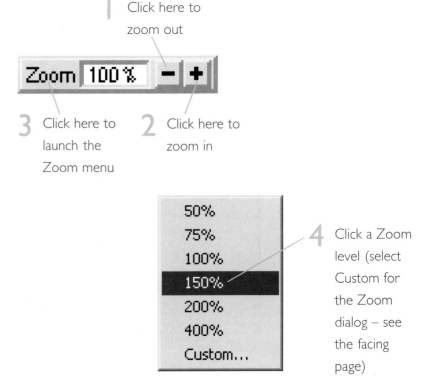

Click here to zoom out

3 Click here to launch the Zoom menu

2 Click here to zoom in

4 Click a Zoom level (select Custom for the Zoom dialog – see the facing page)

Using the Zoom dialog

Using the Zoom dialog, you can perform the following Zoom actions. You can:

Zoom settings have no effect on the way spreadsheets print.

- choose from preset zoom levels (e.g. 200%, 100%, 75%)

- specify your own zoom percentage

If you want to impose your own, custom zoom level, it's probably easier, quicker and more convenient to use the Zoom dialog.

Pull down the View menu and click Zoom. Now carry out step 1 or 2 below. Finally, follow step 3:

2 Click a preset zoom level

Zoom ? X

Zoom enlarges or shrinks the view to show more or less of your document. It does not affect printing.

Specify the magnification to enlarge or shrink the view:

- ○ 400%
- ○ 200%
- ○ 100%
- ○ 75%
- ○ 50%
- ● Custom %: 100

OK   Cancel

1 Type in your own zoom setting (in the range: 25%–1000%)

3 Click here

Selection techniques

Before you can carry out any editing operations on cells in the Spreadsheet module, you have to select them first. Selecting a single cell is very easy: you merely click in it. However, there are a variety of selection techniques which you can use to select more than one cell simultaneously.

Selecting cell ranges with the mouse

The easiest way to select more than one cell at a time is to use the mouse:

Click in the first cell in the range; hold down the left mouse button and drag over the remaining cells. Release the mouse button

Selecting cell ranges with the keyboard

There are two separate techniques you can use:

- Position the cell pointer over the first cell in the range. Hold down Shift as you use cursor keys to extend the selection. Release the keys when the correct selection has been defined

- Position the cell pointer over the first cell in the range. Press F8 to enter Selection mode. Use the cursor keys to define the selection area (see the illustration below). Finally, press F8 again to leave Selection mode

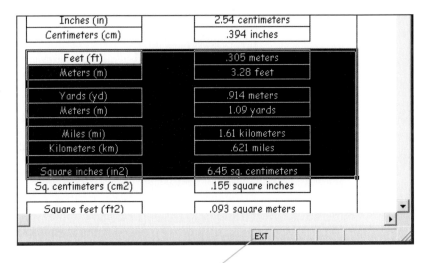

Status bar showing Selection mode in force

Selecting a single row or column

To select every cell within a row or column automatically, click the row or column heading.

Row headings are on the left of the screen (and are expressed as numbers).

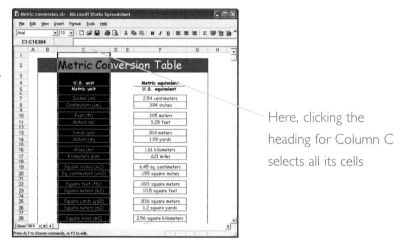

Here, clicking the heading for Column C selects all its cells

Selecting multiple rows or columns

To select more than one row or column, click a row or column heading. Hold down the left mouse button and drag to select adjacent rows or columns.

Selecting an entire spreadsheet

Click the Select All button (or press Ctrl+A):

Select All button

Formulas – an overview

Formulas are cell entries which define how other values relate to each other.

As a very simple example, consider the following:

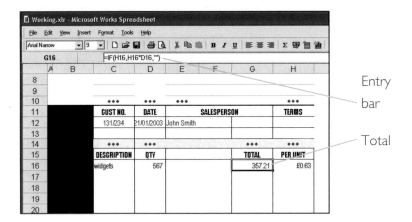

Cell G16 (TOTAL) has been defined so that it multiplies the contents of cells D16 (QTY) and H16 (PER UNIT). Obviously, in this instance you could insert the result easily enough yourself because the values are so small, and because we're only dealing with a small number of cells. But what happens if the cell values are larger and/or more numerous, or – more to the point – if they're liable to change frequently?

The answer is to insert a formula which carries out the necessary calculation automatically.

The 'H16*D16' component tells Works 7 to multiply the contents of the two cells. The 'IF' before the bracket is the conditional operator.

If you look at the Entry bar in the illustration, you'll see the formula which does this:

$$=IF(H16,H16\star D16,"")$$

This is a fairly complex formula. Basically, it instructs Works 7 to inspect cell H16. If an entry is found, the contents should be multiplied by the contents of D16, and the results displayed.

Inserting a formula

All formulas begin with an equals sign. This is usually followed by a permutation of the following:

- an operand (cell reference, e.g. B4)

- a function (e.g. the summation function, SUM)

- an arithmetical operator (+, −, /, * and ^)

- comparison operators (=, <, >, <=, >= and <>)

The Spreadsheet supports a very wide range of functions organised into numerous categories. For more information on how to insert functions, see overleaf.

The mathematical operators are (in the order in which they appear in the bulleted list): *plus, minus, divide, multiply* and *exponential.*

The comparison operators are (in the order in which they appear in the list): *equals, less than, greater than, less than or equal to, greater than or equal to* and *not equal to.*

There are two ways to enter formulas:

Entering a formula directly into the cell
Click the cell in which you want to insert a formula. Then type =, followed by your formula. When you've finished, press Return.

Entering a formula into the Entry bar
Click the cell in which you want to insert a formula. Then click in the Entry bar. Type =, followed by your formula. When you've finished, press Return or do the following in the Entry bar:

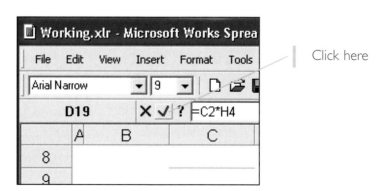

Click here

Functions – an overview

Functions are pre-defined, built-in tools which accomplish specific tasks and then display the result. These tasks are very often calculations; occasionally, however, they're considerably more generalised (e.g. some functions simply return dates and/or times). In effect, functions replace one or more formulas.

The Spreadsheet module organises its functions under the following headings:

- Financial

- Date and Time

- Math and Trigonometry

- Statistical

- Lookup and References

- Text

- Logical

- Informational

Works 7 provides a special shortcut (called Easy Calc) which makes entering functions much easier and more straightforward. Easy Calc is very useful for the following reasons:

- It provides access to a large number of functions from a centralised source

- It ensures that functions are entered with the correct syntax

Functions can only be used in formulas. Note, however, that the result displays in the host cell, rather than the underlying function/ formula.

Displaying/hiding formulas and functions

1 To have Works show formulas and functions (rather than the result) within the cell, pull down the View menu and click Formulas

2 Repeat step 1 to hide formulas/functions

Using Easy Calc

Inserting a function with Easy Calc

At the relevant juncture during the process of inserting a formula, pull down the Tools menu and click Easy Calc. Now do the following:

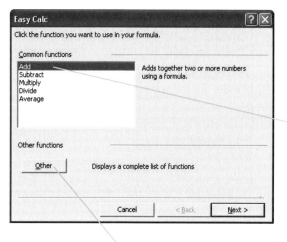

Select a common function then jump to step 5

2 Or, if you need an unusual function, click Other then complete steps 3–8

3 If you followed step 2, select a function type then a specific function on the right

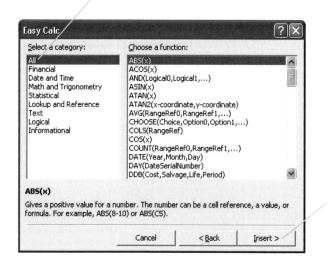

4 Click Insert

Now complete the following dialogs (the contents vary with the function selected):

5 Click the cells (in the spreadsheet) whose values you want to include, or define the appropriate cell range

6 Click here

7 Click the cell (in the spreadsheet) where you want the function stored, or enter its reference

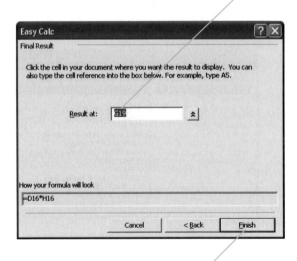

8 Click Finish to insert the function

Spreadsheet protection

If you import spreadsheets in versions of Works which support protection, the protection is removed.

Earlier versions of Works supported protecting individual cells (so that their contents couldn't be overwritten). Works 7, however, does not support this. You can, though, protect the active spreadsheet in its entirety by making it 'read-only'. This level of protection is only valid until someone else removes the read-only tag, so don't use this method to protect sensitive data.

Making spreadsheets read-only

1 Save your spreadsheet in the usual way

2 Launch Windows Explorer or My Computer

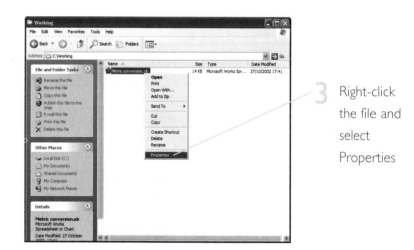

3 Right-click the file and select Properties

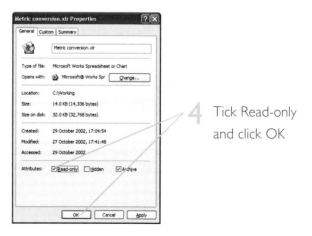

4 Tick Read-only and click OK

Amending row/column sizes

Sooner or later, you'll need to change row or column dimensions when there is too much data in cells to display adequately. You can enlarge or shrink single or multiple rows/columns.

Changing row height

To change one row's height, click the row heading. If you want to change multiple rows, hold down Shift and click the appropriate extra headings. Then pull down the Format menu and click Row Height. Carry out the following steps:

Type in the new height

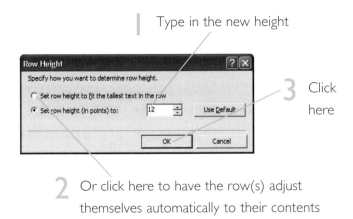

3 Click here

2 Or click here to have the row(s) adjust themselves automatically to their contents

Changing column width

To change one column's width, click the column heading. If you want to change multiple columns, hold down Shift and click the appropriate extra headings. Then pull down the Format menu and click Column Width. Now do the following:

Type in the new height

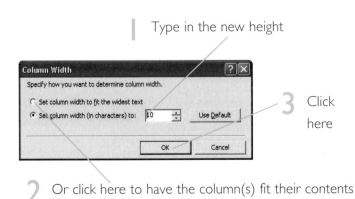

3 Click here

2 Or click here to have the column(s) fit their contents

Inserting rows or columns

You can insert additional rows or columns into spreadsheets.

Inserting a new row or column

First, select one or more cells within the row(s) or column(s) where you want to carry out the insert operation. Now pull down the Insert menu and carry out step 1 OR 2 below, as appropriate:

If you select cells in more than one row or column, Works 7 inserts the equivalent number of new rows or columns.

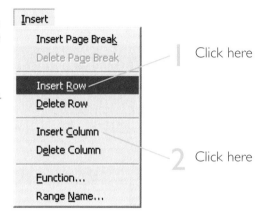

1 Click here

2 Click here

3 The new row(s) or column(s) are inserted immediately:

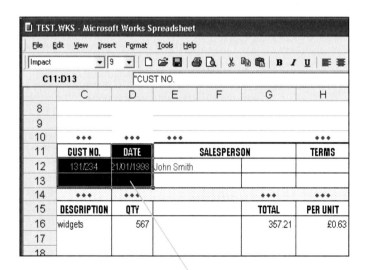

Here, two new columns or three new rows are being added

Working with fills

The Spreadsheet module lets you duplicate the contents of a selected cell down a column or across a row, easily and conveniently. Use this technique to save time and effort.

Duplicating a cell

Click the cell whose contents you want to duplicate. Then move the mouse pointer over the appropriate border; the pointer changes to a cross and the word FILL appears:

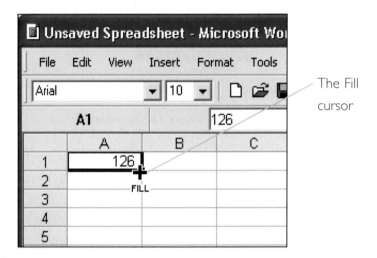

The Fill cursor

Drag the border over the cells into which you want the contents inserted

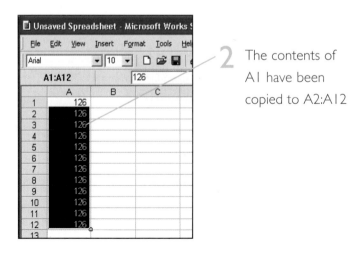

2 The contents of AI have been copied to A2:A12

Using AutoFill

You can also carry out intelligent fills which *extrapolate* cell contents over the specified cells – Works calls these 'data series'. Look at the next illustration:

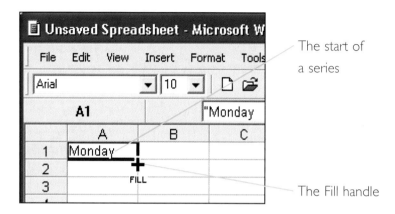

The start of a series

The Fill handle

If (as here) you wanted to insert day names progressively in successive cells in a column, you could do so manually. But there's a much easier way. You can use AutoFill.

Using AutoFill to create a series

Type in the first element(s) of the series in a cell or consecutive cells. Select the cell(s). Then position the mouse pointer over the Fill handle in the bottom right-hand corner of the last cell (the pointer changes to a crosshair). Hold down the left mouse button and drag the handle over the cells into which you want to extend the series. When you release the mouse button, Works 7 extrapolates the initial entry or entries into the appropriate series.

AutoFill also works with gaps in sequences. For example, if you enter Week1 in one cell and Week 4 below it, selecting both cells then dragging the second's Fill handle will produce:

- Week1
- Week4
- Week7
- Week 10

and so on.

The completed series – series can also consist of numbers, months, years and alphanumeric combinations (e.g. Week1, Week 2, Week 3 etc.)

Working with headers/footers

You can print text at the top of each page within a document; the area of the page where repeated text appears is called the 'header'. In the same way, you can have text printed at the base of each page; in this case, the relevant page area is called the 'footer'. Headers and footers are printed within the top and bottom page margins, respectively.

Inserting a header or footer

Pull down the View menu and click Header and Footer. Now do the following as appropriate:

To edit an existing header of footer, amend the text in steps 1 or 2.

You can't alter header or footer formatting at all.

1 Enter header text according to placement

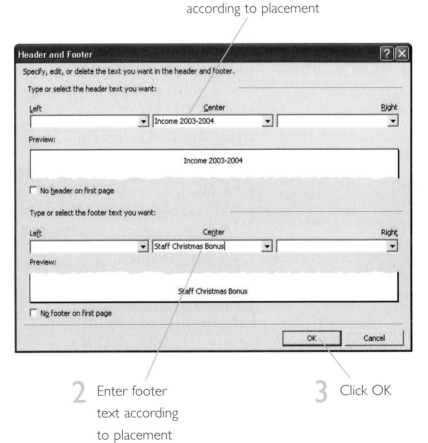

Header and Footer

Specify, edit, or delete the text you want in the header and footer.

Type or select the header text you want:

Left   Center   Right

Income 2003-2004

Preview:

Income 2003-2004

☐ No header on first page

Type or select the footer text you want:

Left   Center   Right

Staff Christmas Bonus

Preview:

Staff Christmas Bonus

☐ No footer on first page

OK   Cancel

2 Enter footer text according to placement

3 Click OK

Viewing headers and footers

1 Pull down the File menu and select Print Preview

2 A header viewed in
Print Preview

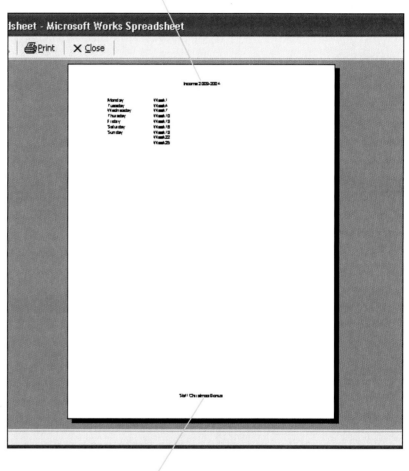

3 A footer viewed in
Print Preview

Changing number formats

The Spreadsheet module lets you apply various formatting enhancements to cells and their contents. You can customise the way cell contents (e.g. numbers and dates/times) display. For example:

- For Fixed, Number, Percent, Currency & Exponential, you can specify the number of decimal places

- For Date & Time, you can specify the format (e.g. 23 August 2003 or 14:23 AM)

- For Fraction, you can specify how fractions are rounded up

- For True/False, General and Text, there are no options

Specifying a number format

1 Select the cells whose contents you want to customise

2 Pull down the Format menu and click Number

3 Ensure the Number tab is active

Works 7 spreadsheets will use Euros as their currency rather than pounds or dollars. Select Currency as the number format then Use the Euro sign...

(You can also insert the Euro symbol – € – manually. Press the Num Lock key. Hold down Alt and press 0128 (consecutively). Release Alt and turn off Num Lock.)

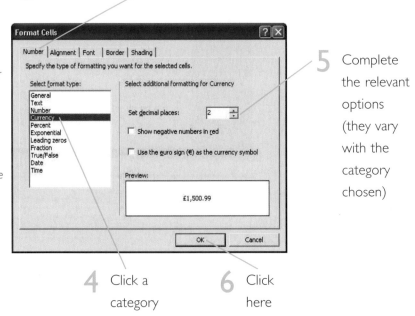

5 Complete the relevant options (they vary with the category chosen)

4 Click a category

6 Click here

Changing fonts and styles

The Spreadsheet module lets you carry out the following actions on cell contents (numbers, text or combinations of both). You can apply:

- a new font

- a new type size

- a font style (*Italic*, **Bold**, Underlining or ~~Strikethrough~~)

- a colour

Amending the appearance of cell contents

Select the cell(s) whose contents you want to reformat. Pull down the Format menu and click Font. Now follow any of steps 1–4 (as appropriate) below. Finally, carry out step 5.

1 Click a font   2 Type in a type size

Re step 4 – you can also select Bold and/or Italic in the Font style field.

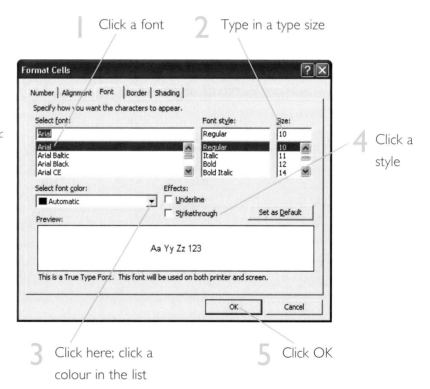

4 Click a style

3 Click here; click a colour in the list

5 Click OK

Cell alignment

By default, Works 7 aligns text to the left of cells, and numbers to the right. However, if you want you can change this.

You can specify alignment under two broad headings: Horizontal and Vertical.

Horizontal alignment

The main options are:

General	the default (see above)
Left	contents are aligned from the left
Right	contents are aligned from the right
Center	contents are centred
Fill	contents are duplicated so that they fill the cell
Center across selection	contents are centred across more than one cell (if you pre-selected a cell range)

Vertical alignment

Available options are:

Top	cell contents align with the top of the cell(s)
Center	contents are centred
Bottom	contents align with the cell bottom

Most of these settings parallel features found in the Word Processor module (and in many other word processors). The difference, however, lies in the fact that in spreadsheets Works 7 has to align data within the bounds of cells rather than a page. When it aligns text, it often needs to employ its own version of text wrap.

See the facing page for more information on this.

By default, when text is too large for the host cell, Works 7 overflows the surplus into adjacent cells to the right. However, you can opt to have the Spreadsheet module force the text onto separate lines within the original cell. This process is called text wrap.

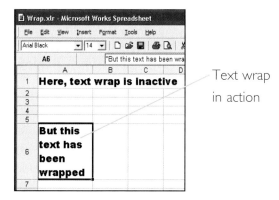

Text wrap in action

Customising cell alignment & applying text wrap

Select the relevant cell(s). Pull down the Format menu and click Alignment. Now follow any or all of steps 1–3 (as appropriate) below. Finally, carry out step 4:

3 Click a vertical alignment

2 Ensure this is ticked to turn on text wrap

1 Click a horizontal alignment

4 Click here

Bordering cells

Works 7 lets you define a border around:

- the perimeter of a selected cell range

- the individual cells within a selected cell range

- specific sides within a cell range

Bordering cells is a useful technique. Reasons you might want to do this include:

- to emphasise cells or cell ranges, and;
- to create individual lines for graphical effect (especially if gridlines are turned off)

You can customise the border by choosing from a selection of pre-defined border styles. You can also colour the border, if required.

Applying a cell border

First, select the cell range you want to border. Pull down the Format menu and click Border. Now carry out steps 1–2 below. Step 3 is optional. Finally, follow step 4:

3 Click a colour

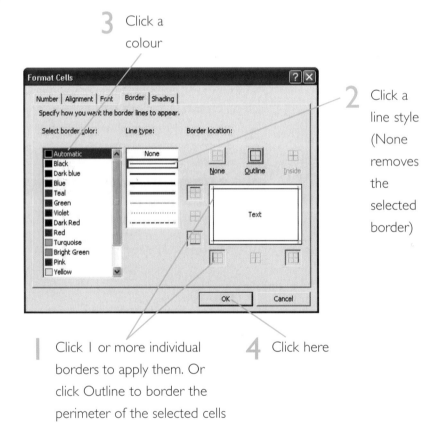

2 Click a line style (None removes the selected border)

1 Click 1 or more individual borders to apply them. Or click Outline to border the perimeter of the selected cells

4 Click here

Shading cells

Works 7 lets you apply the following to cells:

- a pattern

- a foreground colour

- a pattern colour

You can do any of these singly, or in combination. Interesting effects can be achieved by using foreground colours with coloured patterns.

Applying a pattern and/or background

First, select the cell range you want to shade. Pull down the Format menu and click Shading. Now follow steps 1, 2 and/or 3 as appropriate. Finally, carry out step 4:

2 Click a foreground colour

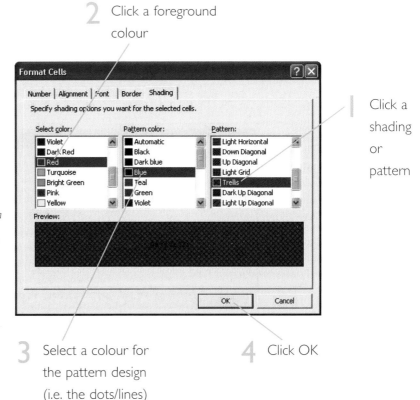

The Preview area shows you how your shading will look.

Click a shading or pattern

3 Select a colour for the pattern design (i.e. the dots/lines)

4 Click OK

AutoFormat

Works 7 provides a shortcut to the formatting of spreadsheet data: AutoFormat.

AutoFormat consists of 19 pre-defined formatting schemes. These incorporate specific excerpts from the font, number, alignment, border and shading options discussed earlier. You can apply any of these schemes (and their associated formatting) to selected cell ranges with just a few mouse clicks. Doing this saves a lot of time and effort, and the results are dependably professional.

AutoFormat works with most arrangements of spreadsheet data. However, if the effect you achieve isn't what you want, you can undo (reverse) AutoFormats by pressing Ctrl+Z immediately after imposing them. (This technique also works with most other Spreadsheet editing actions.)

Using AutoFormat

First, select the cell range you want to apply an automatic format to. Pull down the Format menu and click AutoFormat. Now carry out steps 1 and 2 below:

Select a format

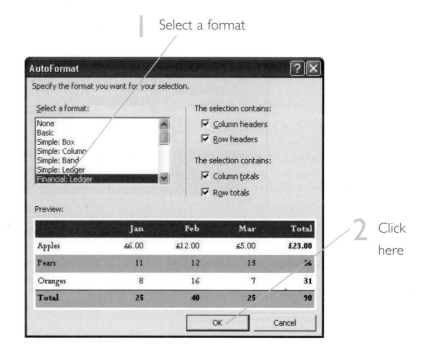

Click here

Find operations

You can search for and jump to text and/or numbers (in short, any information) in your spreadsheets. This is a particularly useful feature when spreadsheets become large and complex, as they almost invariably do.

In Find operations, you can specify whether Works 7 searches:

- by columns or rows

- in cells which contain values (the results of formulas)

- in cells which contain values or formulas

Searching for data

Place the mouse pointer at the location in the active spreadsheet from which you want the search to begin (or, to restrict the search to specific cells, pre-select them). Pull down the Edit menu and click Find. (Or press Ctrl+F.) Now carry out step 1 below, then either of steps 2–3. Finally, carry out step 4:

Type in the data you want to find

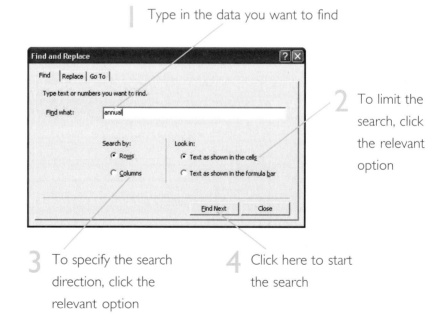

2 To limit the search, click the relevant option

3 To specify the search direction, click the relevant option

4 Click here to start the search

Search-and-replace operations

When you search for data, you can also – if you want – have Works 7 replace it with something else.

Search-and-replace operations can be organised by rows or by columns. However, unlike straight searches, you can't specify whether Works looks in cells which contain formulas or those which don't.

Running a search-and-replace operation
Place the mouse pointer at the location in the active spreadsheet from which you want the search to begin. Pull down the Edit menu and click Replace. Carry out steps 1–3 below. Now do *one* of the following:

- Follow step 4. When Works locates the first search target, carry out step 5 to have it replaced. Repeat this process as often as necessary

- Carry out step 6 to have Works find every target and replace it automatically

If you want to restrict the search-and-replace operation to specific cells, select a cell range before you follow the procedures outlined here.

1 Type in the search data

2 Type in the replacement data

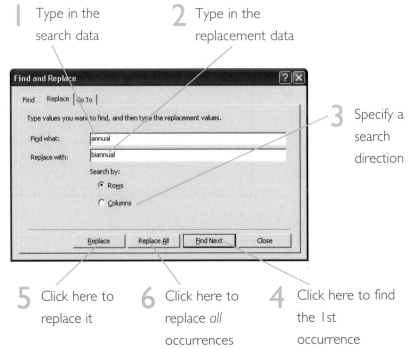

3 Specify a search direction

5 Click here to replace it

6 Click here to replace *all* occurrences

4 Click here to find the 1st occurrence

Charting – an overview

The Spreadsheet module has comprehensive charting capabilities. You can have it convert selected data into its visual equivalent. To do this, Works 7 offers 12 chart formats:

Charts make data more attractive, and therefore easier to take in.

- Area
- Bar
- Line
- Pie
- Stacked Line
- X-Y (Scatter)

- Radar
- Combination
- 3-D Area
- 3-D Bar
- 3-D Line
- 3-D Pie

Works 7 uses a special dialog to make the process of creating charts as easy and convenient as possible.

The illustration below shows a sample 3-D Area chart:

When you create a chart, Works 7 launches it in a separate Chart Editor window.

You can have as many as 8 charts associated with any spreadsheet.

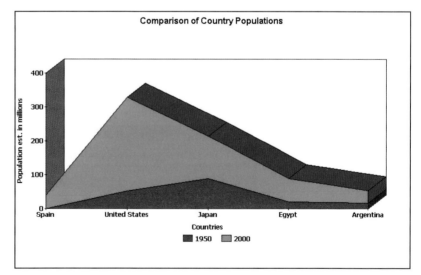

Creating a chart

Select the cells you want to view as a chart. Pull down the Tools menu and click Create New Chart. Carry out steps 1–2 and 6 below. Also follow steps 3–5 if you need to set advanced chart options.

1 Ensure the Basic Options tab is active

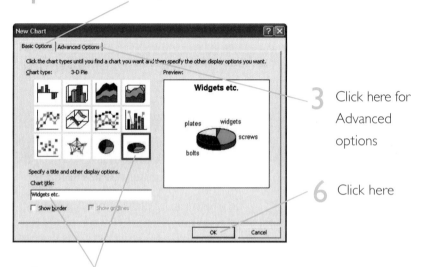

3 Click here for Advanced options

6 Click here

2 Name the chart then select a chart type

4 Complete the advanced fields, as appropriate

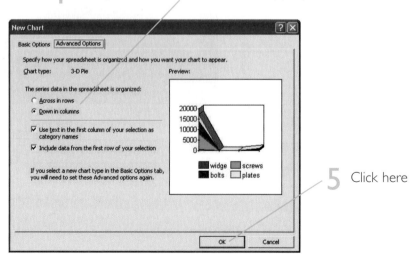

5 Click here

Amending chart formats

Once you've created a chart, you can easily change the underlying chart type. You can also apply a new sub-type.

Each basic chart type has several sub-types (variations) associated with it. These are unavailable when you first create your chart.

Switch to the chart you want to reformat (if it isn't already open, first follow the procedure under 'Viewing charts' on page 117). Pull down the Format menu and click Chart Type. Follow steps 1–2 and 5. If you want to apply a sub-type, also carry out steps 3–4.

1 Ensure the Basic Types tab is active

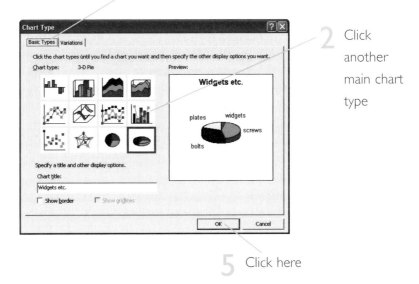

2 Click another main chart type

5 Click here

3 Click the Variations tab

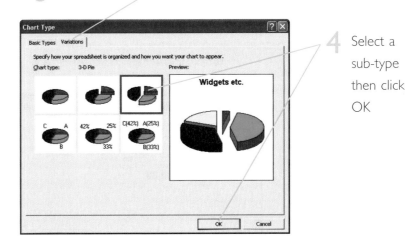

4 Select a sub-type then click OK

Reformatting charts

You can apply a new typeface/type size/font style to chart text or a new colour/shade to graphic components.

Reformatting text

Within the open chart, click the text you want to change. Pull down the Format menu and click Font. Carry out any of steps 1–4, as appropriate. Finally, follow step 5:

The series in a chart are the individual data entries.

1 Select a font

2 Type in a type size

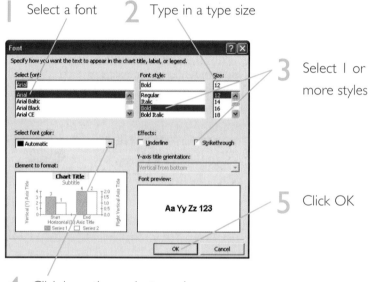

3 Select 1 or more styles

5 Click OK

4 Click here then select a colour

Reformatting graphic objects

Double-click the object (e.g. a series) you want to reformat. Carry out step 1 and/or 2 below. Finally, follow step 3.

Re step 3 – click Format All (instead of Format) to apply the changes to all related value series.

1 Click a colour

2 Click a pattern

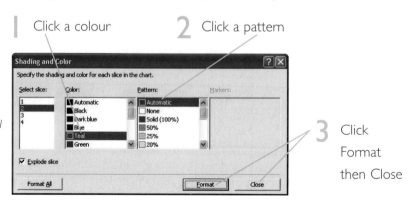

3 Click Format then Close

Chart housekeeping

Viewing charts

A Works 7 spreadsheet can have a maximum of 8 charts associated with it. To view a chart (when Spreadsheet or another chart is on-screen), pull down the View menu and click Chart. Now do the following:

When you've finished working with your chart(s), you can return to the underlying spreadsheet by pulling down the View menu and clicking Spreadsheet.

Click a chart (you can only select one at a time)

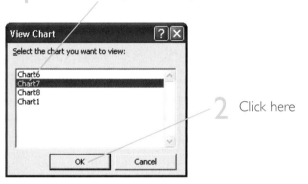

2 Click here

Deleting charts

If you try to create more than 8 charts for a particular spreadsheet, Works 7 will refuse to comply. The answer is to delete one or more unwanted charts.

Follow the procedure above to switch to the chart you want to remove. Pull down the Tools menu and click Delete Chart. Now do the following:

Click a chart

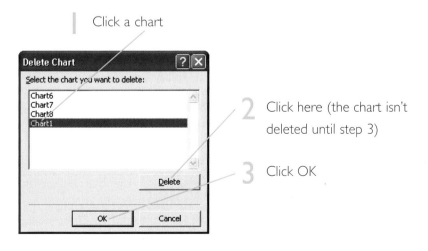

2 Click here (the chart isn't deleted until step 3)

3 Click OK

Page setup

The instructions here and on the facing page also apply to charts.

Making sure your spreadsheets print with the correct page setup can be a complex issue since most eventually won't fit onto 1 page.

The Spreadsheet module comes with 17 pre-defined paper types which you can apply to your spreadsheets, in either portrait (top-to-bottom) or landscape (sideways on) orientation.

Portrait orientation

Landscape orientation

You can also create your own page definitions.

Applying a new page size/orientation

Pull down the File menu and click Page Setup. Now carry out step 1 below, followed by steps 2–3 as appropriate. Finally, carry out step 4:

To create your own paper size, click Custom in step 3. Then type in appropriate measurements in the Height & Width fields.

1 Click this tab 2 Select an orientation

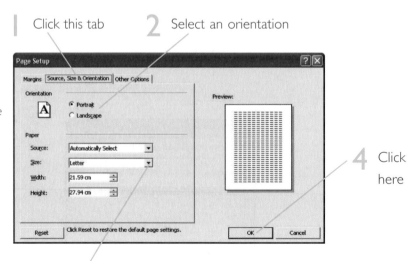

4 Click here

3 Click here and select a page size

Setting margin options

The Spreadsheet module lets you set a variety of margin settings. The illustration below shows the main ones:

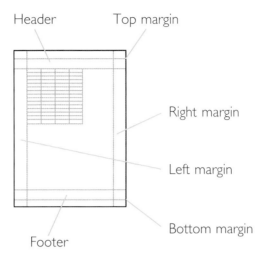

Header   Top margin

Right margin

Left margin

Bottom margin

Footer

Applying new margins

Pull down the File menu and click Page Setup. Now carry out step 1 below, followed by steps 2–3 as appropriate. Finally, carry out step 4:

To specify whether gridlines print (or to set the starting page number), click the Other Options tab. Complete the dialog and click OK.

Click this tab

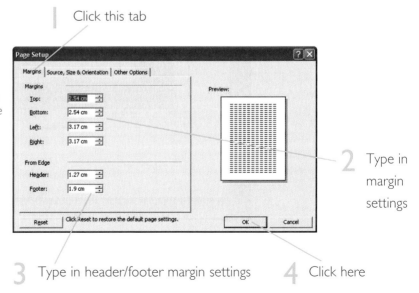

2 Type in margin settings

3 Type in header/footer margin settings

4 Click here

Using Print Preview

You can use an alternative route to preview a chart. Pull down the View menu and click Display as Printed. Works 7 now displays the chart in situ, as it will look when printed. You can go on editing the chart in the usual way.

(Repeat to return to the normal view.)

The Spreadsheet module provides a special view mode called Print Preview. This displays the active spreadsheet (one page at a time) exactly as it will look when printed. Use Print Preview as a final check just before you begin printing.

When you're using Print Preview, you can zoom in or out on the active page. What you can't do, however, is display more than one page at a time or edit the active spreadsheet or chart (in the case of charts, however, see the HOT TIP for a work-round).

Launching/closing Print Preview

1 Pull down the File menu and click Print Preview

2 Click Close in the toolbar (or press Esc) to leave Print Preview

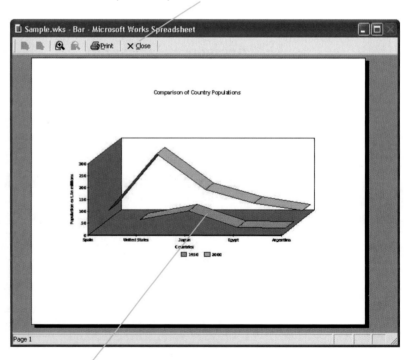

A preview of a
3-D Line chart

Zooming in or out in Print Preview

There are two methods you can use here.

Using the mouse
Do the following:

Repeat step 1 to increase the magnification even more. (Doing so again, however, returns it to the original level.)

Move the mouse pointer over the page and left-click once to zoom in

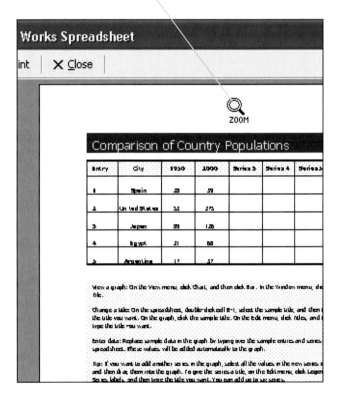

Using the toolbar
Launch Print Preview. Then carry out the following actions:

Click here to zoom in

Click here to zoom out

Changing pages in Print Preview

Although you can only view one page at a time in Print Preview mode, you can step backwards and forwards through Spreadsheet as often as necessary.

There are three methods you can use (in descending order of usefulness).

Using the toolbar
Carry out the following actions:

Click here to move to
the previous page

Click here to move
to the next page

Using the keyboard
You can use the following keyboard shortcuts:

Page Up — Moves to the previous page (in a magnified page view, moves through the current page)

Page Down — Moves to the next page (in a magnified page view, moves through the current page)

Up cursor — Within a magnified view of a page, moves towards the top of the page

Down cursor — Within a magnified view of a page, moves towards the base of the page

Using the scrollbars
When you're working with a magnified view of a page, use the vertical and/or horizontal scrollbars (using standard Windows techniques) to move up or down within the page.

Printing spreadsheet data

When you print your data, you can specify:

You can restrict printing to specific cells by creating a 'print area'. Select the relevant cell range. Pull down the File menu and select Print Area, Set Print Area. In the message, click OK.

(To remove the print area, pull down the File menu and select Print Area, Clear Print Area.)

- the number of copies you want printed

- whether you want the copies 'collated'. This is the process whereby Works 7 prints one full copy at a time. For instance, if you're printing five copies of a 12-page spreadsheet, Works prints pages 1–12 of the first copy, followed by pages 1–12 of the second and pages 1–12 of the third... and so on

- which pages you want printed

- the printer you want to use (if you have more than one installed on your system)

You can 'mix and match' these, as appropriate.

Starting a print run

Open the spreadsheet containing the data you want to print. Then pull down the File menu and click Print. Perform any of steps 1–4. Then carry out step 5 to begin printing:

Click here; select a printer from the list

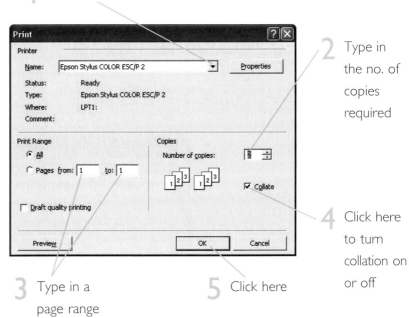

2 Type in the no. of copies required

If you need to adjust your printer's internal settings before you initiate printing, click Properties. Then refer to your printer's manual.

4 Click here to turn collation on or off

Click Draft quality printing to have your spreadsheet print with minimal formatting.

3 Type in a page range

5 Click here

Printing – the fast track approach

In earlier topics, we've looked at how to customise print options to meet varying needs and spreadsheet sizes. However, the Spreadsheet module – like the Word Processor – recognises that there will be times when you won't need this level of complexity. There are occasions when you'll merely want to print out your work (often for proofing purposes):

- bypassing the Print dialog, and;

- with the current print settings applying

For this reason, Works provides a method which is much quicker and easier to use.

Printing with the default print options

1 Open the spreadsheet you want to print

2 Make sure the Toolbar is visible. (If it isn't, pull down the View menu and click Toolbar, Show Toolbar)

3 Click here

4 The active spreadsheet starts to print straightaway

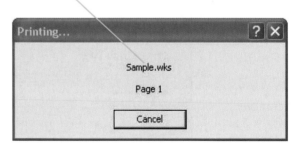

Database

This chapter shows you how to carry out basic/advanced editing in the Database module. You'll learn to work with data and formulas and to move around in databases (including the use of Zoom). You'll also select, locate, sort and filter data, and apply formatting to make it more visually effective. Finally, you'll generate reports, then customise page layout/printing.

Covers

Chapter Four

The Database screen

Below is a detailed illustration of a typical Database screen:

Menu bar   Title bar   Entry bar

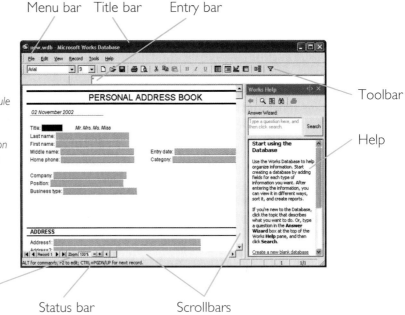

Here, the Database module is displaying in Form view. For more information on Database views, see pages 131–132.

This is the Zoom Area: The screen components here are used to adjust magnification levels. See page 135.

Toolbar

Help

Status bar   Scrollbars

Some of these – e.g. the rulers and scrollbars – are standard to just about all programs which run under Windows. One – the Toolbar – can be hidden, if required.

Specifying whether the Toolbar displays

Pull down the View menu and do the following:

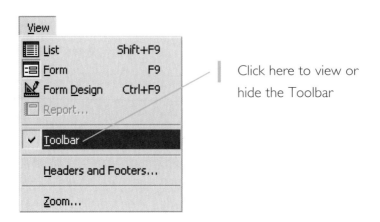

Click here to view or hide the Toolbar

Creating your first database

Unlike the Word Processor and Spreadsheet modules, the Database module doesn't create a new blank document immediately after you've launched it from within the Task Launcher. Instead, you have to complete several dialogs first. Do the following:

1 In the Task Launcher, click the Programs tab. Select Works Database, Start a blank Database

2 Name the 1st field

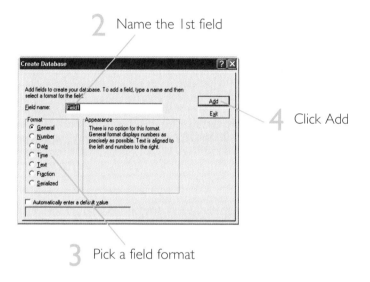

3 Pick a field format

4 Click Add

After you've followed step 4, Works 7 reproduces the same dialog so that you can create the second field. Repeat the above procedures as often as necessary. When you've defined your final field, do the following:

Database fields are single columns of information (in List view) or spaces for the insertion of information (in Form view).

New blank databases automatically appear in List view.

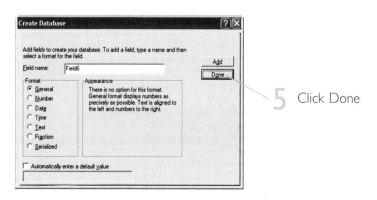

5 Click Done

Entering data

When you've created a database, you can begin entering data immediately. You can enter the following basic data types:

- numbers

- text

- functions

- formulas (combinations of numbers, text and functions)

You enter data into 'fields'. Fields are organised into 'records'. Records are whole units of related information.

To understand this, we'll take a specific example. In an address book, the categories under which information is entered (e.g. Last name, First Name, Home Phone) are fields, while each person whose details are entered into the Database module constitutes one record. This is shown in the next illustration:

In List view, records are shown as single rows. In Form view, only one record displays on-screen at any given time.

For more information on Database views, see pages 131–132.

This is List view. List view is suitable for the mass insertion of data (more than 1 record is visible at a time). However, you can also enter data in Form view.

Fields

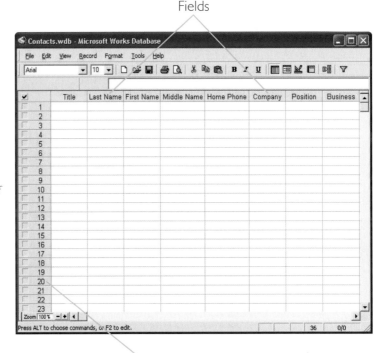

Records

You can insert € *(the Euro symbol) into databases. Fonts which support this include:*

- *Arial*
- *Courier New*
- *Impact*
- *Tahoma, and;*
- *Times New Roman*

To insert the Euro symbol, press the Num Lock key on your keyboard. Hold down Alt and press 0128 (consecutively). Release Alt and turn off Num Lock.

Although you can enter data *directly* into a database field (by simply clicking in it and typing it in), there's another method you can use which is often easier. Like the Spreadsheet module, the Database module provides a special screen component known as the Entry bar.

In the illustration below, two fields in the first record have been completed.

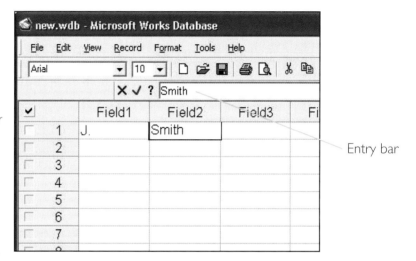

Entry bar

Entering data via the Entry bar

Click the field you want to insert data into. Then click the Entry bar. Type in the data. Then follow step 1 below. If you decide not to proceed with the operation, follow step 2 instead:

Click here (or press Enter)

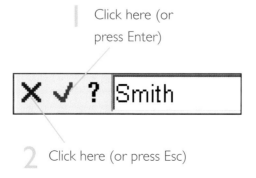

2 Click here (or press Esc)

Modifying existing data

You can amend the contents of a field in two ways:

- via the Entry bar

- from within the field itself

When you use either of these methods, the Database module enters a special state known as Edit Mode.

In-cell editing may be disabled. To restore it, pull down the Tools menu and click Options. In the Options dialog, select the Data Entry tab and tick Edit in cells and in entry bar. Click OK.

Amending existing data using the Entry bar

Click the field whose contents you want to change. Then click in the Entry bar. Make the appropriate revisions and/or additions. Then press Return. The relevant field is updated.

Amending existing data internally

Click the field whose contents you want to change. Press F2. Make the appropriate revisions and/or additions *within the field*. Then press Return.

The illustration below shows our new database, in Form view.

The first record

This is Form view before any formatting enhancements have been applied – for an idea of what a more developed Form view looks like, see the illustration on the facing page.

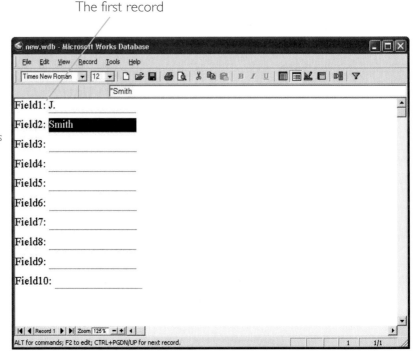

Using Database views

The Database module provides two principal views:

List

List view presents data in a grid structure reminiscent of the Spreadsheet module – the columns denote fields and the rows individual records. Pictures and most formatting do not display.

Use List view for bulk data entry or comparison.

Form

Form view only displays one record at a time but presents it in a way which is easier on the eye. The basis of this view is the 'form', the underlying layout which you can customise in Form Design view. Pictures and formatting display (although you can only initiate or modify them in Form Design view).

Form view is often the best way to interact with your database.

Form Design view is a subset of Form view. (For how to use Form Design view, see pages 143 and 148–151).

There are two further view modes: Report (see pages 158–159) and Print Preview (see pages 160–162).

A database in Form view...

The same database in List view...

You can use three methods to switch to another view.

The menu approach...

Pull down the View menu and do the following:

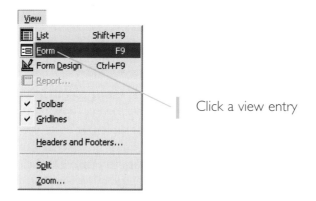

Click a view entry

If the Toolbar isn't currently on-screen, pull down the View menu and click Toolbar.

The Toolbar approach...

Refer to the Toolbar. Now click one of the following:

List view   Form Design view

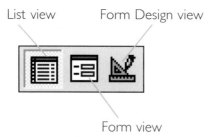

Form view

The keyboard approach...

You can also use the following keyboard shortcuts:

F9   Form view

Shift+F9   List view

Ctrl+F9   Form Design view

Moving around in databases

Databases can quickly become very large. The Database module provides several techniques you can use to find your way round.

Using the scrollbars

Use any of the following methods:

1. To scroll quickly to another record (in List view) or to another field (in Form view), drag the scroll box along the Vertical scrollbar until you reach it

2. To move one window to the right or left, click to the left or right of the scroll box in the Horizontal scrollbar

3. To move one window up or down, click above or below the scroll box in the Vertical scrollbar

4. To move up or down by one record (in List view) or one field (in Form view), click the arrows in the Vertical scrollbar

5. To move left or right by one field, click the arrows in the Horizontal scrollbar

Scroll box

Scroll arrow

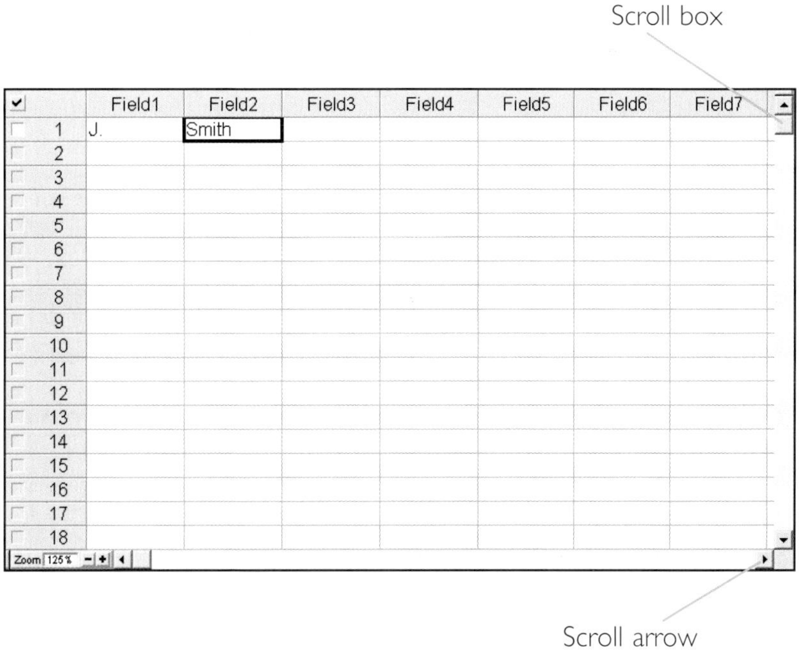

Using the keyboard

You can use the following techniques:

1. In List view, use the cursor keys to move one field left, right, up or down. In Form or Form Design views, use the up and left cursor keys to move one field up, or the down and right keys to move one field down

2. Press Home to jump to the first field in the active record, or End to move to the last

3. Press Ctrl+Home to move to the first record in the open database, or Ctrl+End to move to the last

4. Press Page Up or Page Down to move up or down by one screen

5. In Form or Form Design views, press Ctrl+Page Down to move to the next record, or Ctrl+Page Up to move to the previous one

Using the Go To dialog

The Database module provides a special dialog which you can use to specify precise field or record destinations.

In any view, pull down the Edit menu and click Go To (or press F5). Now carry out step 1 OR 2 below. Finally, follow step 3.

2 Type in a record number

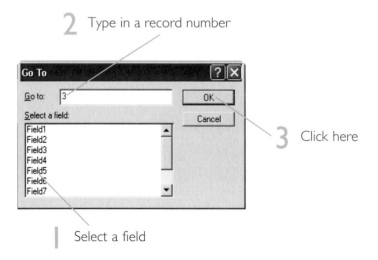

3 Click here

Select a field

Using zoom

The ability to vary the level of magnification in the Database module is very useful. Sometimes, it's helpful to 'zoom out' (i.e. decrease the magnification) so that you can take an overview; at other times, you'll need to 'zoom in' (increase the magnification) to work in greater detail. Works 7 makes this process easy and convenient.

You can change magnification levels in the Database module:

* with the use of the Zoom Area

* with the Zoom dialog

Using the Zoom Area

You can use the Zoom Area (in the bottom left-hand corner of the screen) to alter zoom levels with the minimum of effort. Carry out step 1 or 2, or steps 3–4, as appropriate:

Click here to zoom out

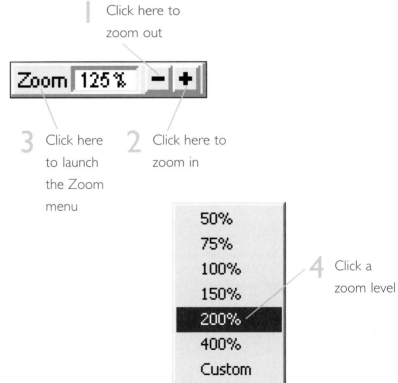

Click here to zoom in

Click here to launch the Zoom menu

Re step 4 – clicking Custom produces the Zoom dialog (you can also launch this by selecting Zoom in the View menu). Do one of the following:

* *select a preset zoom level (e.g. 75% or 200%), or;*
* *enter your own zoom level in the Custom field (in the range 50–1000%)*

Finally, click OK.

Click a zoom level

Selection techniques in List view

Before you can carry out any editing operations on fields or records in the Database module, you have to select them first. The available selection techniques vary according to whether you're currently using List, Form or Form Design view.

In List view, follow any of the techniques below:

Using the mouse

To select a single field	Simply click in it
To select multiple fields	Click the field in the top left-hand corner; hold down the mouse button and drag over the fields you want to highlight. Release the mouse button
To select one record	Click the record number
To select several records	Hold down Shift as you click their record numbers

With the exception of the first, selected fields are filled with black.

✔		Surname	First Name	Address1	Address2	Phone Number
☐	1	Smith	John	19 High Street	Anytown	01044 887235
☐	2	Brown	Ian	46 Chorely Avenue	Anytown	0912 66543
☐	3	Green	Brian	82 The Drive	Padiham	01234 897345
☐	4	Smith	John	19 High Street	Anytown	01044 887235

Record numbers

Using the keyboard

To select the whole of the active database in List view, press Ctrl+Shift+F8.

To select multiple fields	Position the insertion point in the first field. Press F8 to enter Selection mode ('Ext' displays in the Status bar). Use the cursor keys to extend the selection area. Press F8 when you've finished
To select a whole record	Position the insertion point in the record. Press Ctrl+F8
To select a whole field	Position the insertion point in the field. Press Shift+F8

Selection techniques in forms

Using the mouse

To select a single field   Simply click in it

To select multiple fields   Hold down Ctrl as you click in successive fields (you must be in Form Design view to do this)

To select one record   Click any of the following:

These arrow buttons can be found in the bottom left-hand corner of the Form and Form Design view screens.

To previous record   To final record

To first record   To next record

To select multiple field names or inserted pictures   In Form Design view, hold down the Ctrl key as you click successive objects

Several fields selected in Form Design view

Using the keyboard

To select a field   Use the cursor keys to position the insertion point in the relevant field

To select a record   Press Ctrl+Page Up or Ctrl+Page Down until the record you want is displayed

Formulas – an overview

You can insert formulas into Database fields. Formulas in the Database module work in much the same way as in the Spreadsheet. However, there are fewer applications for them.

Database formulas serve two principal functions:

• to ensure that the same entry appears in a given field throughout every record in a database

• to return a value based on the contents of multiple additional fields

Look at the next illustration:

The formula/function appears in the Entry bar

For the NOW() function to return a date as its result, the host field must have had the Date number format applied to it – see page 141.

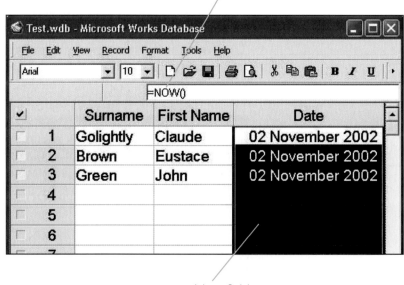

New field

Here, an extra field has been added (see page 141 for how to do this) and a formula (in this case, consisting entirely of a function) inserted. The function:

=NOW()

inserts the current system date in the Date field within every record (you can vary the format).

Inserting a formula

Arguments (e.g. field references) relating to functions are always contained in brackets.

As in the Spreadsheet module, all Database formulas must begin with an equals sign. This is usually followed by a permutation of the following:

- one or more operands (in the case of the Database module, field names)

- a function (e.g. AVG – returns the Average)

- an arithmetical operator $(+, -, /, \star$ and $\char"5E$ $)$

The Database module supports a very wide assortment of functions. For how to insert functions, see overleaf.

The arithmetical operators are (in the order in which they appear in the bulleted list above):

plus, minus, divide, multiply and *exponential*.

There are two ways to enter formulas:

Entering a formula directly into the field
Click the field into which you want to insert a formula. Then type =, followed by your formula. When you've finished defining the formula, press Return.

The Entry bar method is usually the most convenient.

Entering a formula into the Entry bar
Click the field in which you want to insert a formula. Then click in the Entry bar. Type =, followed by your formula. When you've finished defining the formula, press Return or:

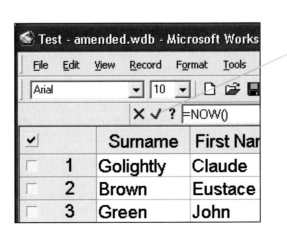

Click here

Inserting a function

In many ways, the Database module's implementation of functions parallels that of the Spreadsheet module. However, there is one important difference: you can't use Easy Calc to insert them. Instead, you have to do so manually.

There are two ways to insert functions:

Entering a function directly into the field

Re step 3 – as an example, if you're entering the AVG function (which returns the average of selected fields), type in the field details (arguments) e.g. to average fields called Week1 and Week2, type:

=AVG(Week1,Week2)

1 Click the field into which you want to insert the function

2 Type = followed by the function itself – e.g. =NOW()

3 Don't forget to include any arguments – see the HOT TIP

4 Press Enter

Entering a function into the Entry bar

If you need help with inserting a function, pull down the Help menu and click Contents. Select Calculate with Formulas and Functions. Select Work with Database Functions then Use Database Functions. Now select a function type (e.g. Use Financial Functions) then a specific function.

1 Click the field into which you want to insert the function

2 Click in the Entry bar; type = followed by the function itself

3 Don't forget to include any arguments – see the HOT TIP

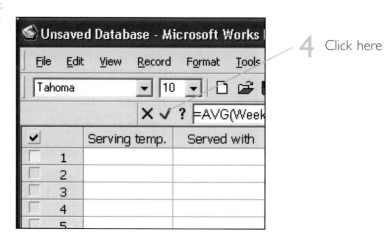

4 Click here

Inserting fields

Adding a field in Form Design view

1 If you're not already in Form Design view, pull down the View menu and click Form Design

2 Click where you want the new field inserted then pull down the Insert menu and click Field

3 Name the new field

Re step 4 – most of the number formats you can choose from are identical to those used in the Spreadsheet module.

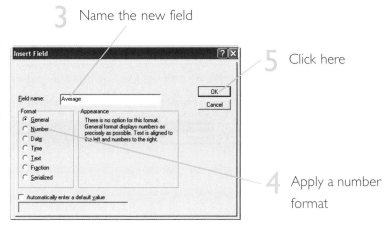

5 Click here

4 Apply a number format

Adding one or more fields in List view

To edit an existing field, select it in List or Form Design view. Pull down the Format menu and select Field. Complete the dialog.

1 If you're not currently in List view, pull down the View menu and click List

2 Click in the field (column) next to which you want the new field(s) added

3 Pull down the Record menu and click Insert Field. In the sub-menu, click Before or After, as appropriate

4 Carry out steps 3–4 above then click Add to create the new field

5 Repeat step 4 as required then click Close

Inserting records

You can add one or more blank records to the active database, from within either Form (but not Form Design) or List view.

Adding a record in Form view

If you're not already in Form view, pull down the View menu and click Form. Go to the record (see page 134) before which you want the new record to appear. Pull down the Record menu and click Insert Record.

If you select more than one existing record (by holding down Shift as you click the relevant row headings), Works 7 inserts the equivalent number of new records.

Adding a record in List view

If you're not currently in List view, pull down the View menu and click List. Click in the record above which you want the new record added. Pull down the Record menu and click Insert Record.

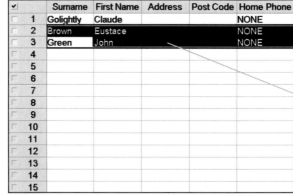

✔		Surname	First Name	Address	Post Code	Home Phone
☐	1	Golightly	Claude			NONE
☐	2	Brown	Eustace			NONE
☐	3	Green	John			NONE
☐	4					
☐	5					
☐	6					
☐	7					
☐	8					
☐	9					
☐	10					
☐	11					
☐	12					
☐	13					
☐	14					
☐	15					

Preparing to add two new records in List view

To hide one record in Form view, go to it. In List view, however, select one or more records. Now in either case pull down the Record menu and click Hide Record.

To make all records visible again, pull down the Record menu and click Show All Records.

✔		Surname	First Name	Address	Post Code	Home Phone
☐	1	Golightly	Claude			NONE
☐	2					
☐	3					
☐	4	Brown	Eustace			NONE
☐	5	Green	John			NONE
☐	6					
☐	7					
☐	8					
☐	9					
☐	10					
☐	11					
☐	12					
☐	13					
☐	14					
☐	15					

The records have been added

Using clip art

You can insert clip art into databases, but only in Form Design view.

Inserting clip art into Form Design view

1   If you're not already in Form Design view, press Ctrl+F9

2   Insert your copy of the Works 7 CD into the drive

3   Ensure no item is selected

Clip art is visible in Form (but not List) view.

4   Pull down the Insert menu and click Clip Art

5   Select a category   7   Select a clip

6   Select a sub-category   8   Click Insert

9   For more information on clip art and how to use it, see pages 54–58

Amending record/field sizes

Sooner or later, you'll find it necessary to change the dimensions of fields or records within List view. This necessity arises when there is too much data to display adequately. You can enlarge or shrink single or multiple fields/records.

Changing record height

To change one record's height, click the record number. If you want to change multiple records, hold down Shift and click the appropriate extra numbers. Then pull down the Format menu and click Record Height. Carry out the following steps:

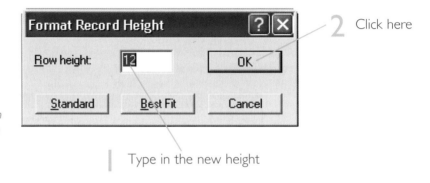

2 Click here

Type in the new height

Click Best Fit in either dialog to have the record(s) or field(s) adjust themselves automatically to their contents.

Changing field widths

To change one field's width, click the field heading. If you want to change multiple fields, hold down Shift and click the appropriate extra headings. Then pull down the Format menu and click Field Width. Now do the following:

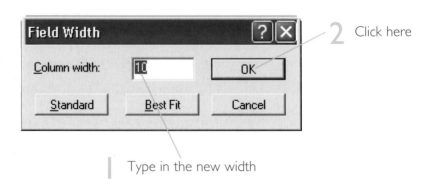

2 Click here

Type in the new width

Working with fills

In List view, you can have the contents of a selected field entry automatically copied into other field entries or records.

Duplicating a field entry

Click the field whose contents you want to duplicate. Then select the fields or records into which you want the contents inserted

✔		Surname	First Name	Post Code	Home Phone
☐	1	Golightly	Claude		NONE
☐	2	Brown	Eustace		
☐	3	Green	John		
☐	4				
☐	5				
☐	6				
☐	7				
☐	8				
☐	9				
☐	10				
☐	11				
☐	12				
☐	13				
☐	14				
☐	15				

The contents of the Home Phone field in record I will be copied into the same field in records 2–3

Pull down the Edit menu and click Fill Right or Fill Down, as appropriate

✔		Surname	First Name	Post Code	Home Phone
☐	1	Golightly	Claude		NONE
☐	2	Brown	Eustace		NONE
☐	3	Green	John		NONE
☐	4				
☐	5				
☐	6				
☐	7				
☐	8				
☐	9				
☐	10				
☐	11				
☐	12				
☐	13				
☐	14				
☐	15				

The fill operation has been completed

Working with fill series

You can also carry out fills which *extrapolate* field entry contents over the specified entries. You could do this manually, of course, but Works 7 provides a much easier way. You can insert a series.

Creating a series

Type in the first element(s) of the series in 1 or more consecutive fields

✔		Surname	First Name	Month
☐	1	Golightly	Claude	January
☐	2	Brown	Eustace	
☐	3	Green	John	
☐	4			
☐	5			
☐	6			
☐	7			
☐	8			

2 Select the original field(s) and those you want the series extended into. Pull down the Edit menu and click Fill Series

✔		Surname	First Name	Month
☐	1	Golightly	Claude	January
☐	2	Brown	Eustace	
☐	3	Green	John	
☐	4			
☐	5			
☐	6			
☐	7			
☐	8			

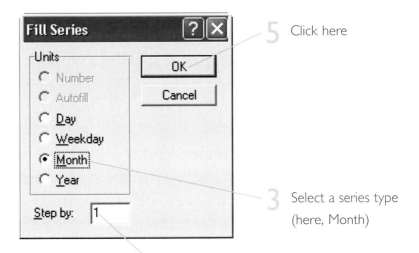

5 Click here

3 Select a series type (here, Month)

4 Type in a step value (plus numbers for increments, minus numbers for decrements). -2 in this instance would produce: November, September, July, May, March, January...

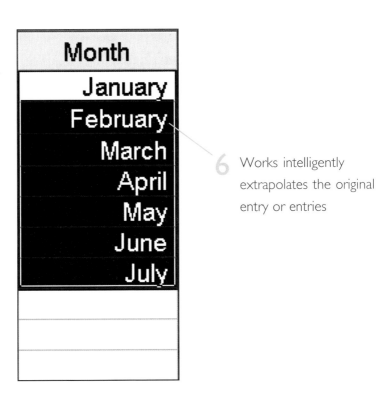

6 Works intelligently extrapolates the original entry or entries

Changing fonts and styles

The Database module lets you carry out the following actions on field contents (numbers, text or combinations of both). You can:

• apply a new font

• apply a new type size

• apply a font style (*Italic*, **Bold**, Underline or ~~Strikethrough~~)

• apply a colour

Amending the appearance of field contents

Select the data you want to reformat. Pull down the Format menu and click Font and Style. Now follow any of steps 1–4, as appropriate. Finally, carry out step 5.

1 Select a font

2 Type in a type size

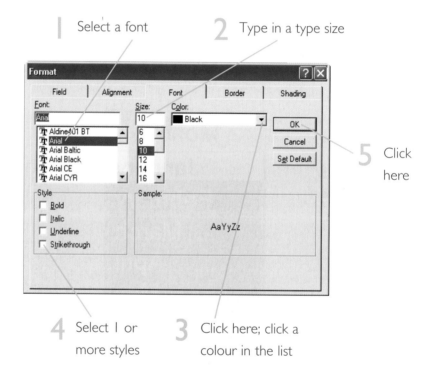

5 Click here

4 Select 1 or more styles

3 Click here; click a colour in the list

Aligning field contents

You can apply the following alignments to field entries:

Horizontal alignment

General   the default (text to the left, numbers to the right)

Left   contents are aligned from the left

Right   contents are aligned from the right

Center   contents are centred

The horizontal alignment options are available in both List and Form Design views. The vertical alignment options, however, are unavailable in Form Design view.

Vertical alignment

Top   contents align with the top of the field(s)

Center   contents are centred

Bottom   contents align with the base of the field(s)

Customising alignment & applying text wrap

Select the relevant field(s). Pull down the Format menu and click Alignment. Now follow any or all of steps 1–3, as appropriate. Finally, carry out step 4.

This is the List view version of the dialog.

Re step 3 – in List view, select Wrap text to have surplus text within a field forced onto separate lines within it.

In Form Design view, select Slide to left to have Works 7 change the field height to accommodate text.

2 Click a vertical alignment

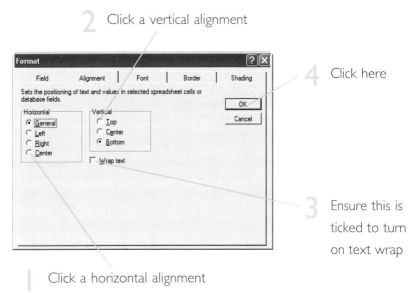

4 Click here

3 Ensure this is ticked to turn on text wrap

Click a horizontal alignment

Bordering fields

You can border fields in Form Design view, too, but to a lesser extent.

In List view, you can define a border around:

- the perimeter of selected field(s)

- the individual fields *within* a group of selected fields

- specific field sides

You can customise the border by choosing from a selection of pre-defined border styles. You can also colour it, if required.

Applying a field border

First, click the heading(s) of the field(s) you want to border. Pull down the Format menu and click Border. Now carry out steps 1 and 2 below. Step 3 is optional. (If you're setting multiple border options, repeat steps 1–3 as required). Finally, carry out step 4:

Re step 1 – Outline is only available in Form Design view and borders the perimeter of the selected field(s). The other options (you can select more than 1) are only available in List view and affect individual sides.

1 Select the extent of the border (see the HOT TIP)

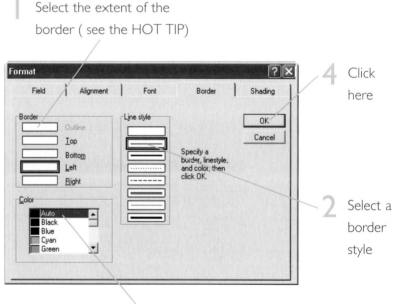

4 Click here

2 Select a border style

3 Select a border colour

Shading fields

In List view, you can apply the following to fields:

- a pattern

- a foreground colour

- a pattern colour

You can apply these effects in Form Design view, too, but with one proviso: if no fields have been pre-selected they apply to the whole of the form (and the dialog below is slightly different).

You can do any of these singly, or in combination. Interesting effects can be achieved by using foreground colours with coloured patterns.

Applying a pattern or background

First, select the heading(s) of the field(s) you want to shade. Pull down the Format menu and click Shading. Now carry out step 1 below. Follow step 2 as appropriate. Finally, carry out step 3:

Select a shading
or pattern

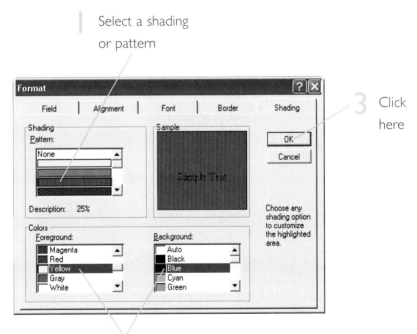

3 Click here

2 Select a colour for the pattern design (i.e. the dots/lines) then select a background colour

Find operations

In List or Form views, you can search for text and/or numbers. There are two basic options. You can:

- have the first matching record display

- view all records which contain the specified text or numbers

Searching for data

Pull down the Edit menu and click Find (or press Ctrl+F). Now carry out step 1 below, then *either* step 2 or 3. Finally, carry out step 4:

1 Type in the data you want to find

3 Or click here to view *all* matching records

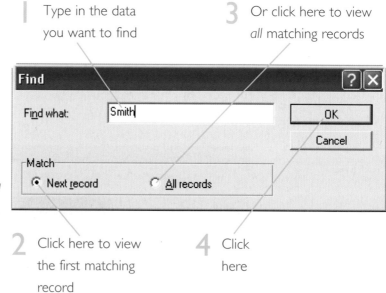

If the Find dialog does not allow you to carry out a precise enough search, use filters instead – see page 154.

2 Click here to view the first matching record

4 Click here

Showing all records again

1 If you followed step 3 above, Works 7 will only display matching records (other records in your database are inaccessible)

2 To show all records again, pull down the Record menu and click Show, All Records

Search-and-replace operations

When you search for data, you can also – if you want – have Works 7 replace it with something else – but only in List view.

You can specify the following search directions:

Records   the search is left-to-right

Fields   the search is top-to-bottom

Running a search-and-replace operation

Pull down the Edit menu and click Replace (or press Ctrl+H). Carry out steps 1–3 below. Now do *one* of the following:

• Follow step 4. When Works locates the first search target, carry out step 5 to have it replaced. Repeat this process as often as necessary

• Carry out step 6 to have Works find *every* target and replace it automatically

Type in the data you want to find

4 Click here to find the 1st occurrence

5 Click Replace

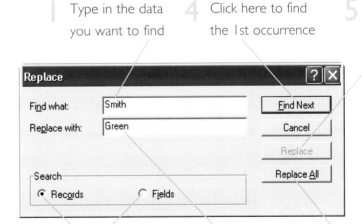

3 Specify the search direction

2 Type in the replacement data

6 Click here to replace *all* occurrences

Using sorts/filters

Sorting data

In Form or List view, you can sort database data alphanumerically.

1 Pull down the Record menu and click Sort Records

2 Select the field you want to sort by

If you also want to sort by subsidiary fields, follow these procedures for either or both Then by: fields.

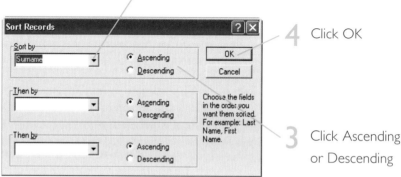

4 Click OK

3 Click Ascending or Descending

Filtering data

Filters determine which records are viewed.

1 Pull down the Tools menu and click Filters

To cancel the effects of filters, pull down the Record menu and select Show, All Records.

2 In the Filter Name dialog, name the filter and click OK

3 Select a field and then a comparison

4 Enter match values

Repeat – if applicable – for additional fields below the first (remembering to select AND or OR in the box to the left) as a way of further refining the filter.

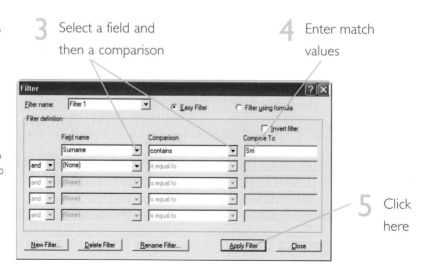

5 Click here

Page setup

The Database module comes with 8 pre-defined paper types which you can apply to your databases, in either portrait (top-to-bottom) or landscape (sideways on) orientation.

Portrait orientation

Landscape orientation

If none of the supplied page definitions is suitable, you can create your own.

Applying a new page size/orientation

Pull down the File menu and click Page Setup. Now carry out step 1 below, followed by steps 2–3 as appropriate. Carry out step 4:

Ensure this tab is active

To create your own paper size, click Custom Size in step 2. Then type in the relevant measurements in the Height & Width fields.

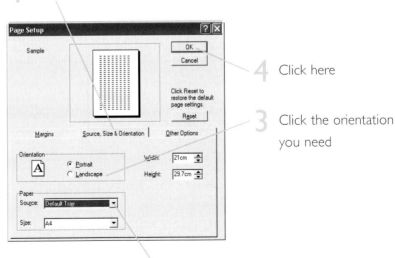

Click here

Click the orientation you need

Click here and select a page size

Setting margin options

The Database module lets you set a variety of margin settings. The illustration below shows the main ones:

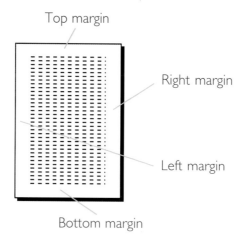

Top margin

Right margin

Left margin

Bottom margin

Applying new margins

Pull down the File menu and click Page Setup. Now carry out step 1–3 below:

Ensure the Margins tab is active

Optionally, type in header or footer margin settings in the Header margin or Footer margin fields.

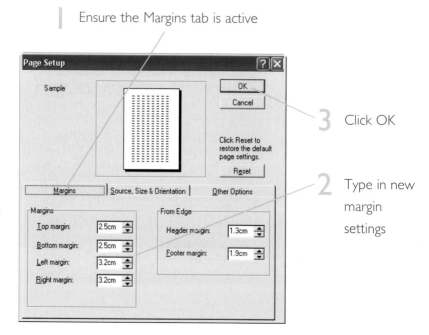

3 Click OK

2 Type in new margin settings

Other page setup options

You can determine whether gridlines and record/field headings print. These are demonstrated below:

Field heading   Gridline

	Surname	First Name	Address1	Address2
1	Smith	John	19 High Street	Anytown
2	Brown	Ian	46 Chorely Avenue	Anytown
3	Green	Brian	32 The Drive	Padiham
4	Smith	John	19 High Street	Anytown
5	Brown	Ian	46 Chorely Avenue	Anytown
6	Green	Brian	32 The Drive	Padiham
7	Smith	John	19 High Street	Anytown
8	Brown	Ian	46 Chorely Avenue	Anytown
9	Green	Brian	32 The Drive	Padiham
10	Smith	John	19 High Street	Anytown

Record heading

Printing gridlines and record/field headings

Pull down the File menu and click Page Setup. Now carry out step 1 below, followed by step 2 as appropriate. Finally, carry out step 3:

This is the List view version of the dialog. There are extra options when you launch it in other views – for example, you can opt to have all records on new pages and you can specify the gap between records.

You can also set the page number for the first page in your database – just type it into the Starting page number: field.

Ensure this tab is active

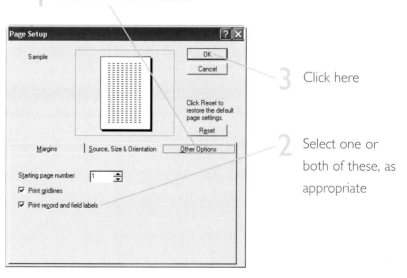

3 Click here

2 Select one or both of these, as appropriate

Report creation

You can use ReportCreator to compile a report according to the criteria you set. You can specify:

- the report name and title

- which fields are included

- the order in which fields are arranged ('sorting')

- which records are included ('filtering')

When a report has been generated, Works 7 stores it in a special view mode called Report Definition. This resembles List view but has labelled rows, not numbered records.

Creating a report

1 Pull down the Tools menu and click ReportCreator

2 Name the report (up to 15 characters)

3 Click here

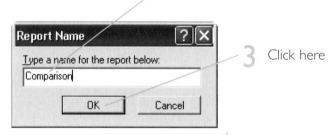

4 Type in a title (up to 255 characters)

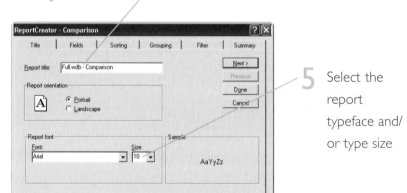

5 Select the report typeface and/ or type size

6 Work through the remaining dialog tabs, making any appropriate choices. For example, to specify the fields which are to be included in the report, click here then follow step 7

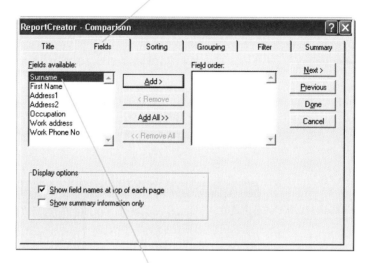

7 Double-click the field(s) you want to include

8 When you've finished customising the report, click Done

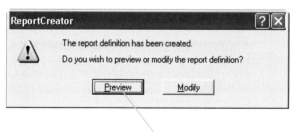

9 Click Preview to view your report in Print Preview

Using Print Preview

The Database module provides a special view mode called Print Preview. This displays the active database (one page at a time) exactly as it will look when printed. Use Print Preview as a final check just before you begin printing.

To view an existing report in Print Preview, pull down the View menu and click Report. In the View Report dialog, double-click a report.

When you're using Print Preview, you can zoom in or out on the active page. What you can't do, however, is:

- display more than one page at a time

- edit or revise the active database

Launching Print Preview

Pull down the File menu and click Print Preview. This is the result:

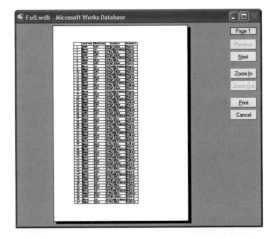

A database in List view, viewed in Print Preview (the Control Panel is on the right)

To leave Print Preview and return to your database, press Esc.

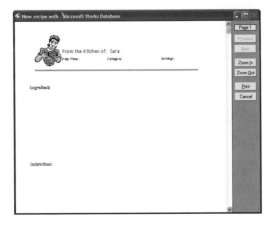

A database in Form view, viewed in Print Preview and with the Zoom level increased

Zooming in or out in Print Preview

Using the mouse

Repeat step 1 to increase the magnification even more. (Doing so again, however, returns it to the original level.)

Move the mouse pointer over the page and left-click once to zoom in

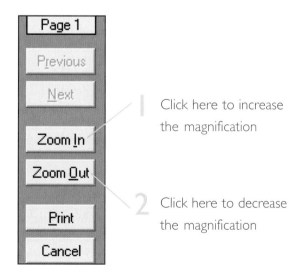

Surname	First Name	Address1	Address2
Smith	John	19 High Street	Anytown
Brown	Ian	46 Chorely Avenue	Anytown
Green	Brian	32 The Drive	Padiham
Smith	John	19 High Street	Anytown
Brown	Ian	46 Chorely Avenue	Anytown
Green	Brian	32 The Drive	Padiham
Smith	John	19 High Street	Anytown
Brown	Ian	46 Chorely Avenue	Anytown
Green	Brian	32 The Drive	Padiham

Using the Control Panel

Launch Print Preview. Then refer to the Control Panel in the top right-hand corner of the screen and do one of the following:

Click here to increase the magnification

Click here to decrease the magnification

Changing pages in Print Preview

Although you can only view one page at a time in Print Preview mode, you can step backwards and forwards through the Database module as often as necessary.

There are three methods you can use :

Using the Control Panel

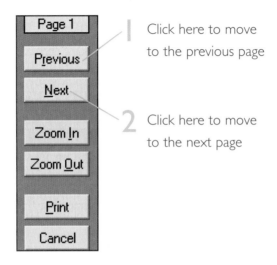

1 Click here to move to the previous page

2 Click here to move to the next page

Using the keyboard
You can use the following keyboard shortcuts:

Page Up	Moves to the previous page (in a magnified page view, moves through the current page)
Page Down	Moves to the next page (in a magnified page view, moves through the current page)
Up cursor	Within a magnified view of a page, moves towards the top of the page
Down cursor	Within a magnified view of a page, moves towards the base of the page

Using the scrollbars
When you're working with a magnified view of a page, use the vertical and/or horizontal scrollbars (using standard Windows techniques) to move up or down within the page.

Printing database data

When you print your data, you can specify:

- the number of copies you want printed

- whether you want the copies 'collated'. This is the process whereby Works 7 prints one full copy at a time. For instance, if you're printing five copies of a 12-page spreadsheet, Works prints pages 1–12 of the first copy, followed by pages 1–12 of the second and pages 1–12 of the third... and so on

- which pages you want printed

- the printer you want to use (if you have more than one installed on your system)

For fast-track printing using the dialog defaults, click the Print button in the Toolbar.

You can 'mix and match' these, as appropriate.

Starting a print run

Open the database containing the data you want to print. Then pull down the File menu and click Print. Perform any of steps 1–4. Then carry out step 5 to begin printing:

To select a printer or set its properties, click here

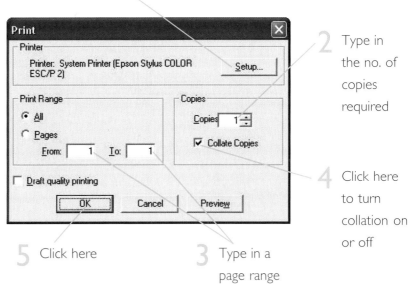

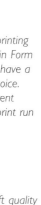

If you're printing from within Form view, you have a further choice. Click Current record only to limit the print run to the active record.

Click Draft quality printing to have your spreadsheet print with minimal formatting.

2 Type in the no. of copies required

4 Click here to turn collation on or off

5 Click here

3 Type in a page range

Printing marked records

You can also use another technique to print specific records.

Marking and then printing records

1 If you're not already in List view, press Shift+F9

2 Tick those records you want to print

✔		Surname	First Name	Address1
☐	1	Smith	John	19 High Street
☐	2	Brown	Ian	46 Chorely Avenue
☐	3	Green	Brian	82 The Drive
✔	4	Smith	John	19 High Street
✔	5	Brown	Ian	46 Chorely Avenue
✔	6	Green	Brian	82 The Drive
✔	7	Smith	John	19 High Street
✔	8	Brown	Ian	46 Chorely Avenue
✔	9	Green	Brian	82 The Drive
☐	10	Smith	John	19 High Street
☐	11	Brown	Ian	46 Chorely Avenue
☐	12	Green	Brian	82 The Drive
☐	13	Smith	John	19 High Street
☐	14	Brown	Ian	46 Chorely Avenue
☐	15	Green	Brian	82 The Drive

Select Show, Unmarked Records instead if you want to print those records you haven't flagged.

3 In List or Form view, pull down the Record menu and click Show, Marked Records

✔		Surname	First Name	Address1
✔	4	Smith	John	19 High Street
✔	5	Brown	Ian	46 Chorely Avenue
✔	6	Green	Brian	82 The Drive
✔	7	Smith	John	19 High Street
✔	8	Brown	Ian	46 Chorely Avenue
✔	9	Green	Brian	82 The Drive
☐	91			
☐	92			
☐	93			
☐	94			
☐	95			
☐	96			
☐	97			
☐	98			
☐	99			

4 The unmarked records are hidden

5 Print in the normal way (see page 163)

Calendar

This chapter shows you how to organise your busy schedule with the Calendar module. You'll learn how to view specific dates; switch to different views; and insert appointments and events. You'll go on to make appointments and events recurring, locate specific examples, set alarms and apply filters as a way of restricting which items display.

Finally, you'll use the Task Launcher to view appointments and events; update your Calendar in line with your portable device and print out your Calendar.

Covers

Chapter Five

Calendar – an overview

You can use the Calendar module to:

- track appointments

- track events

- set alarms which remind you of important appointments/ events

- make appointments etc. recurring

Printing

To print the Calendar, pull down the File menu and click Print. Now do the following:

1   Click here; select a style

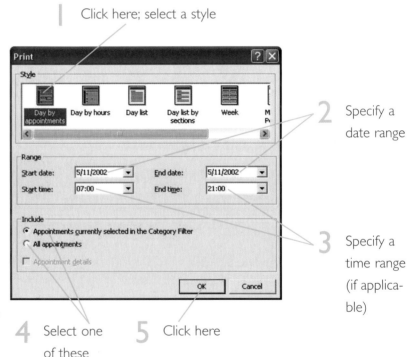

2   Specify a date range

3   Specify a time range (if applicable)

4   Select one of these

5   Click here

Re step 4 – select Appointments currently selected in the Category Filter to print only pre-selected appointments (see page 169).

6   Complete the standard Print dialog which now launches then click OK

The Calendar screen

Below is an illustration of the Calendar screen:

Menu bar   Title bar   Toolbar

Here, the Calendar is displaying one day only, split into its component hours. This is called Day View. There are two other views. Week View shows a 7-day week, starting from Monday, while Month View shows every day in the given month.

To change the view, pull down the View menu and select Day, Week or Month.

Help

Current date

Appointment window

Jumping to dates

To view new dates, pull down the Edit menu and click Go To, Date. (Alternatively, press Ctrl+G.) Now do the following:

| Enter a date (or click the arrow and select one from the drop-down calendar)

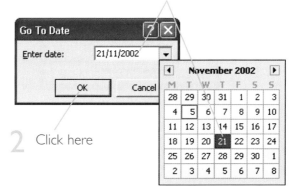

2 Click here

Using the Home Page Calendar

The Calendar module now has a presence on the Task Launcher, so you can see when appointments are due even more readily.

1 Launch the Task Launcher in the usual way

2 Select Home in the menu bar then refer to the right of the Task Launcher

3 Choose a month and day

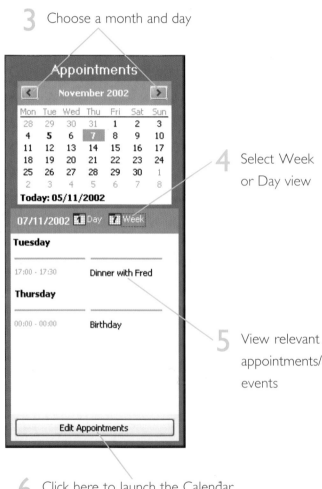

4 Select Week or Day view

5 View relevant appointments/ events

6 Click here to launch the Calendar module - select an appointment or event for editing in the normal way

Entering appointments

In Day view, double-click the day for which you want to enter the appointment. Do the following:

To apply a category to your new appointment, click the Change button. Categories are used by filters – see below.

Name the appointment

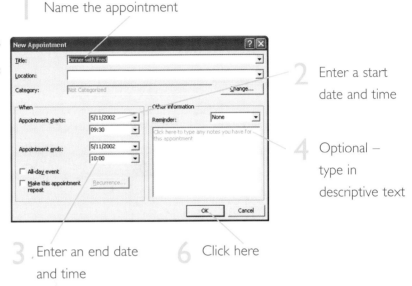

2 Enter a start date and time

4 Optional – type in descriptive text

3 Enter an end date and time

6 Click here

When you apply a filter, you display only those appointments which have had a specific category or categories applied to them.

5 To make an appointment recurring, select Make this appointment repeat. Click Recurrence and complete the dialog

Applying filters

Pull down the View menu and click Show Category Filter. Then:

To view all appointments again, pull down the View menu and click Category Filter, Show appointments in all categories.

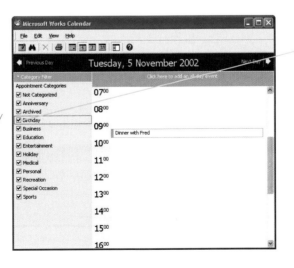

Untick categories relating to appointments you don't want to view

Appointment management

Editing appointments

1 In any Calendar view, double-click an appointment

2 Carry out steps 1–5 on page 169, as appropriate

3 Additionally, to set up an alarm click in the Reminder button

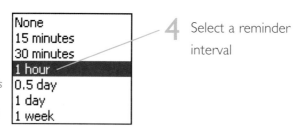

4 Select a reminder interval

5 A bell appears next to the appointment:

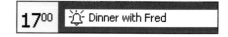

6 Finally, perform step 6 on page 169

Moving appointments

1 In the appropriate Calendar view, drag an appointment to a new date and/or time

Deleting appointments

1 Right-click an appointment – in the menu, select Delete Item

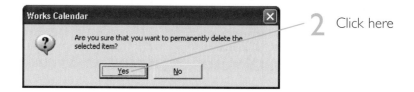

2 Click here

Entering events

You can track events. While appointments relate to a specific time (e.g. a meeting), events either do not (e.g. a birthday) or are spread out over more than one day (e.g. holidays or conferences).

Creating an event

Select Week view and do the following:

To edit an existing event, double-click it in any view then complete the dialog.

Events can also be moved and deleted just like appointments.

 Double-click the day you want the event to start

2 Name the event

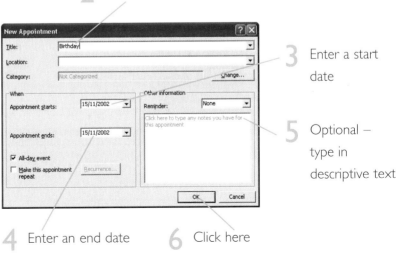

3 Enter a start date

5 Optional – type in descriptive text

Just like appointments, events can be made recurring or have alarms imposed.

4 Enter an end date

6 Click here

Synchronisation

You can synchronise data between the Calendar module and Pocket PCs or Windows CE devices. This means that any changes you make to your calendar, in Works or on your portable device, are automatically updated in the other (even if Works is not running when you connect your portable device to your PC).

Synchronising with your portable device

1 Ensure ActiveSync has been installed on your PC and your portable device is attached to it in line with the manufacturer's instructions

2 Launch the Task Launcher in the usual way

3 Select Tasks   5 Select a portable device then click Start this task

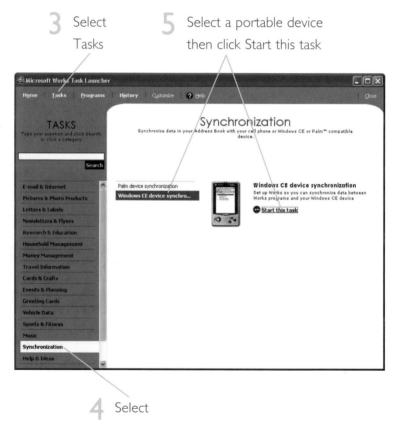

4 Select Synchronization

6 Follow the on-screen instructions

Works Portfolio

Works Portfolio is a great way to organise text, graphics and sounds. You'll learn how to create collections of these in Portfolio and then retrieve them when you need to insert content into your Works documents.

You'll also switch between Portfolio views, manage collections, email them to other people and print them out directly from within Works Portfolio.

Covers

Chapter Six

Works Portfolio – an overview

Works Portfolio is a specialised module you can use to store text, picture and sound files. You can then draw on this convenient repository of information when you create documents in other modules.

There are two basic operating modes: Compact view and Gallery view. The first operates as a small on-screen icon you can use to launch the various features, the second is a full-screen view.

Starting Works Portfolio

1 Start the Task Launcher in the usual way

2 Click Programs

4 Click a Portfolio option

3 Click Works Portfolio

5 Click Start this task

Portfolio views

You can use Works Portfolio full-screen or as a pull-down icon.

Compact view

There is also a third view: Docked. In Docked view, Works Portfolio is fixed on the right of the screen and the drop-down section of Compact view is permanently visible.

Double-click any item in Compact or Docked view to add a descriptive comment. (In Gallery view, enter it directly in the Comments field.)

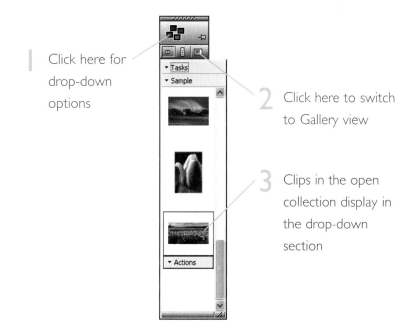

Click here for drop-down options

2 Click here to switch to Gallery view

3 Clips in the open collection display in the drop-down section

Gallery view

Click here to switch to Compact view

2 Clips display here

Using collections

Works Portfolio operates via collections. You can create as many context-related collections as you want and store text or picture items in them. For example, you may want to create one collection relating to your job, another for photographs from your digital camera and one more for pictures or files sent to you via email...

You can rename or delete collections. In any view, click the Tasks button and make a choice.

Creating a new collection

Works Portfolio comes with one small collection called Sample – this displays automatically. You can use this for experimentation but it's best to create your own collections.

1 In Compact view, click the Title bar to launch the drop-down section then press Ctrl+N

2 In Docked or Gallery view, press Ctrl+N

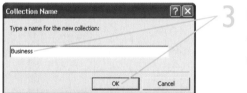

3 Name the collection then click OK

4 The new (empty) collection

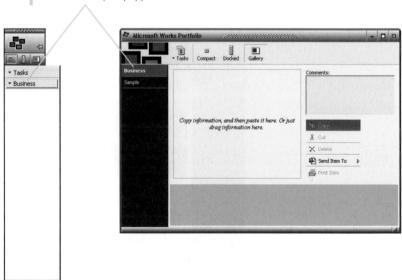

Adding items to collections

Using drag-and-drop

With programs (like Word 2002) which support drag-and-drop, this is the easiest way to get content into your collections.

You can insert files directly into Works Portfolio (but you can't print them). In any view, click the Tasks button and select Insert File.

1   In Works Portfolio, click the appropriate collection button

2   In the host program, select text or a graphic

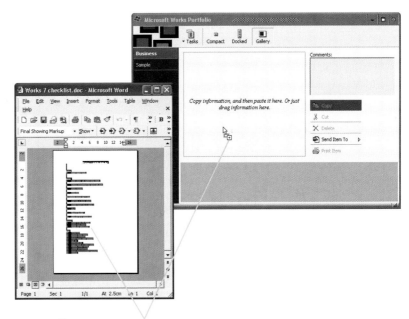

3   Drag the selected item (here, a Word document) onto Works Portfolio – if you drag it onto the Compact version, the drop-down area launches

Using copy-and-paste

If you're copying items on a Web page into Works Portfolio, don't select the whole of the page – this may mean the information fails to copy.

1   In Works Portfolio, click the appropriate collection button

2   In the host program, select the text or picture and press Ctrl+C

3   In any incarnation of Works Portfolio, press Ctrl+V

Using collection items

You can insert collection items into any Works (or just about any other) document.

Using drag-and-drop

1 In Works Portfolio, click the appropriate collection button

2 Drag an item into a Word Processor, Spreadsheet or Database document

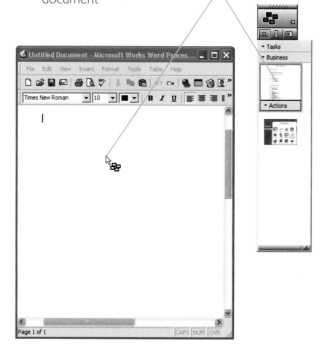

Using copy-and-paste

In Compact or Docked view, you can pre-select more than one item for copying – see step 2 on page 180.

1 In Works Portfolio, click the appropriate collection button

2 Right-click an item

3 In the menu, click Copy

4 In the Works document, press Ctrl+V or Shift+Insert

Sending Portfolio items

The Works Portfolio is a useful base from which to email items or collections. You can also send them for inclusion in Works tasks.

Sending items

1 Select a collection

You can also send entire collections. Click the Tasks button. In the menu, select Send Collection To, E-mail or Works Task.

2 Select an item

3 Select Send Item To, E-mail or Works Task

4 If you selected E-mail in step 3, your email program launches with text inserted into the body of the new email or picture(s) inserted as an attachment

5 If you selected Works Task in step 3, double-click a task in the Pick a task dialog. Works launches the task then prompts you to drag-and-drop the item into it

Printing

You can print items or collections (but not inserted files) directly from within Works Portfolio.

Printing items

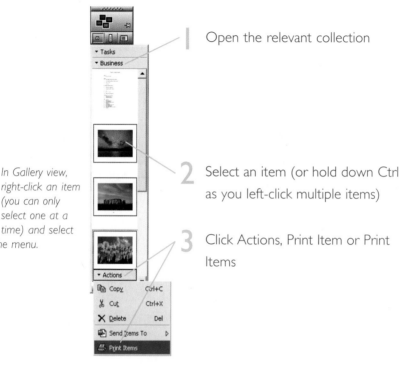

In Gallery view, right-click an item (you can only select one at a time) and select Print Item in the menu.

1 Open the relevant collection

2 Select an item (or hold down Ctrl as you left-click multiple items)

3 Click Actions, Print Item or Print Items

4 Printing is immediate

Printing collections

1 In Compact view, click the Title bar

2 In any view, click the Tasks button

3 In the menu, select Print Current Collection

4 Printing begins straightaway

My Projects Organizer

My Projects Organizer is a great way to ensure any jobs ('projects') you have to perform are carried out promptly and correctly. You'll learn how to create blank projects with your own steps ('To Dos') then use prepared projects for common tasks.

You'll also add comments to To Dos and associate Works 7 tasks, modules or Web links with them. Then you'll action To Dos, so Works launches the appropriate task/module and you can work on it straightaway. Finally, you'll mark finished To Dos as completed and open your projects from the Task Launcher.

Covers

Chapter Seven

An overview

My Projects Organizer is a Works module that you can use to plan out and organise projects. You do this by creating blank projects and adding your own To Dos (individual steps which you can allocate a deadline to) or you can use prepared projects. Works 7 provides a variety of these, so there's a good chance you'll find one which is close to your requirements. Examples of prepared projects include planning a journey, setting up a party and moving to a new house.

The projects you create can be any task/job you have to carry out.

Starting My Projects Organizer

1 Start the Task Launcher in the usual way

2 Click Programs

4 Click Start a Blank Project

3 Click My Projects Organizer

5 Or select a prepared project then click Start this task

Creating a blank project

The value of creating your own projects is that it forces you to think about how best to achieve your objectives.

If you followed steps 1–4 on the facing page, do the following:

2 Name the project

4 Click here then enter To Do details

3 Enter a project deadline

5 Save your project

Click the icon to the immediate left of the Due Date field to insert a note into a To Do.

6 Repeat step 4 for as many To Dos as you need

Also, if appropriate, allocate a deadline to each To Do.

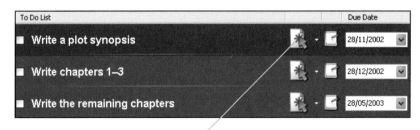

7 For each To Do, click this icon

*Re step 8 –
Works may
suggest a Web
link. If no Web
links appear and
you want to use your own, click
Associate a Web site link on the
left of the screen, after the To
Do has been created. Complete
the dialog and click OK.*

8 If one of the suggested tasks
is appropriate, click it

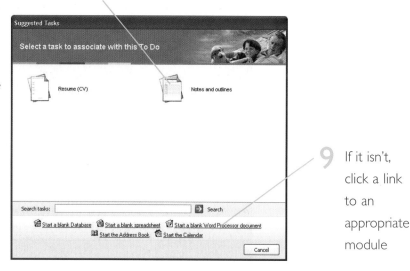

9 If it isn't,
click a link
to an
appropriate
module

10 To start working on a To Do, double-click it

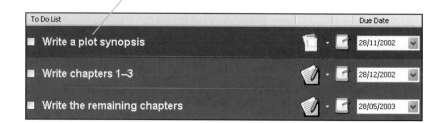

11 If you allocated a task to the To Do in step 8, Works launches
the relevant module complete with the associated wizard.
Choose a document type in the wizard, click Finish then work
on the new document

12 If you allocated a module to the To Do in step 9, Works
launches the relevant module with a blank document. Work
on this

Working with prepared projects

See also page 186 for how to open your own projects you've worked on earlier.

Don't forget to save your work.

If you followed steps 1–3 and 5 on page 182, do the following:

2 Use the techniques described earlier to amend any of the To Dos in line with your requirements

3 Double-click a To Do to action it

4 Works launches a task or module. (Or, as here, a Web link)

Completing projects

Completing a To Do

To print out a list of To Dos, click Print To Do List on the left of the screen then complete the Print dialog.

1 When a To Do has been completed, tick this

Using the Task Launcher

My Projects Organizer has a presence on the Task Launcher, so it's even easier to launch projects.

1 Click Home

You can also open projects by clicking Open a project on the left of the screen and completing the Open dialog.

2 Click Works Projects then launch a prepared project

3 Or click the My Projects tab and launch a project you've created

Index

E

F

G

T

V

W